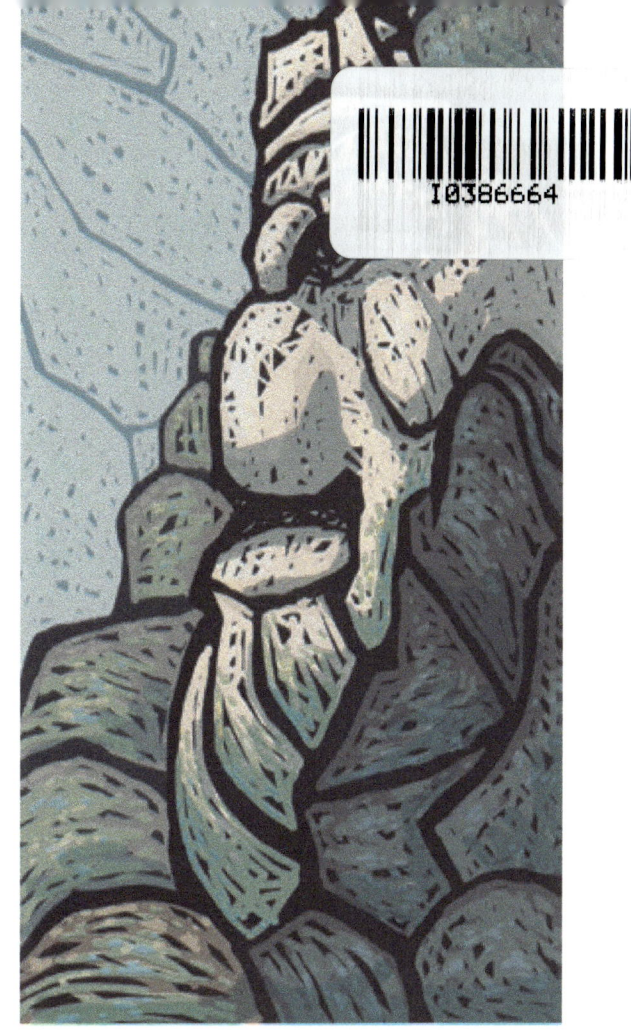

THE CITY OF NEPHI
The Navel of the World
The Center of the Universe

L. (Les) Norman Shurtliff

Cover Picture (underlined)
Inside Picture (underlined)
Artist rendition of the face of Wiracochan, The Son of God

Nephi with the Sword of Laban standing near the entrance gate of the Fortress of Sacsahuaman, north of Cusco (defensive resort for the City of Nephi). Nephi lived and ruled this capital city from approximately 590 B.C. to his death in 545 B.C.

ISBN 978-1-956001-96-9 (paperback)
ISBN 978-1-956001-97-6 (eBook)

Copyright © 2020 by L. (Les) Norman Shurtliff

All rights reserved. No part of this publication may be reproduced, distributed, or transmitted in any form or by any means, including photocopying, recording, or other electronic or mechanical methods without the prior written permission of the publisher.

Printed in the United States of America

CONTENTS

List of Pictures 4
List of Figures 7
Acknowledgements 9
Dedication 9
Preface 10
Chapter 1 – Introduction 13
Chapter 2 – Truths 21
Chapter 3 – Legends 29
Chapter 4 – Travels of Nephi 59
Chapter 5 – Book of Mormon Geography 73
Chapter 6 – Basic Theories 111
Chapter 7 – Characteristics of The City of Nephi 139
Chapter 8 – City of Cusco, Peru 155
Chapter 9 – Temple of Nephi 193
Chapter 10 – Temple of Koricancha 209
Chapter 11 – Summary 239
Bibliography 244
About The Author 246

LIST OF PICTURES

Facing Picture for Chapter #1 12
Facing Picture for Chapter #2 20
Facing Picture for Chapter #3 28
Facing Picture for Chapter #4 58
Facing Picture for Chapter #5 72
Facing Picture for Chapter #6 110
Facing Picture for Chapter #7 138
Facing Picture for Chapter #8 154
Facing Picture for Chapter #9 192
Facing Picture for Chapter #10 208
Facing Picture for Chapter #11 238

1. Ancient Incan Record Keeping 14
2. Wiracochan's Image 31
3. Statue of Pizarro 34
4. Mount Pinkuylluna 37
5. Wiracochan wakes up 39
6. Wiracochan eyes light up 39
7. Beautiful Colors in Textiles 41
8. Pisac and Condor Mountain 47
9. Tree of Life – Nazca Line 48
10. A typical Village Plaza 51
11. Actual Picture of the Tree of Life 54
12. Manco Capac overlooking his Cusco 65
13. Volcanic Mountain Peaks 83
14. Llama – A Domesticated Cameloid 92
15. Vicunas – A wild Cameloid only for Peruvian Royalty 93
16. Peruvian man dyeing wool 96
17. Pre-Inca Agricultural Reserve 99
18. Native woman weaving 101
19. Map of South America Mountain Ranges 109

20. Migrations by Reed Boats 114
21. Native craftsmen on Lake Titicaca 115
22. Large Reed Boats last for many years 119
23. Pyramid of Pacaritanpu 129
24. Ruins of Tambomachay 130
25. Ruins of Machu Pichu 132
26. Walls of the Temple of Koricancha 135
27. Reed Islands of Lake Titicaca 136
28. Native girl weaving 144
29. View of city from the Fortress of Sacsahuaman 146
30. There are several possible tunnel entrances 148
31. Ancient City of Cusco as a Puma 156
32. View of Modern City of Cusco 158
33. Inca Road 164
34. Picture of Francisco Pizarro 169
35. Plaza de Armas 174
36. Fortress of Sacsahuaman 175
37. Massive fortress stonework 176
38. Circular Tower Foundation 178
39. Two More Tower Foundations 179
40. Tunnel beneath Avenue of the Sun 181
41. Modern City of Cusco 184
42. World famous ruins of Machu Pichu 187
43. New Archaeological Dig 188
44. Woman using foot plough 189
45. Typical Peruvian woman 191
46. Interior Temple courtyard 195
47. Temple Block in Cusco 197
48. Walls are larger at base 200
49. Golden Temple of Koricancha before Pizarro 210
50. Two rooms of the temple 213
51. From Steps of Santo Domingo Chapel 214

52. Temple of Koricancha with Chapel on top 215
53. Interior of Temple with Alter Stone 217
54. Santo Domingo pillar and arch on Temple Wall 219
55. Beautiful Temple is a famous tourist spot.................................221
56. Inside the Temple of Koricancha..223
57. Temple Walls are leaning 224
58. Outer Wall of temple..226
59. Famous temple gardens and fountains 227
60. The famous 'Eternity Windows' 228
61. Close up of round wall 232
62. Outer wall of temple and terraces 235
63. Large Massive stones exquisitely dressed 236
64. Carved face of Wiracochan on the mountain...........................242

LIST OF FIGURES

Source Document #1 – Church Archives Document 22
Introduction Map #1 – Chapter #2 – Truths 27
1. Artist's Representation of Wiracochan 38
2. Artist's Rendition of Condor 47
3. Diagram of the Tree of Life 49
4. Ideogram of Custodial Trees 50
5. The Lehi Stone 52
6. Artist's Rendition of the Tree of Life 53
7. Inca Quipu System of Knots 55
8. Map of Arabian Peninsula 64
9. Lehi's Landing and Nephi's Trek 69
10. Map of Ocean's Currents 79
11. Map of Present Day South America 81
12. Map of South America Before Christ 82
13. Map of Andean Mountains 88
14. Basic Mental Image of Book of Mormon 91
15. Inca Roads 91
16. Non-Qualifying Isthmuses 103
17. Complete Map of Narrow Neck of Land 105
18. Map of Geography of the Book of Mormon 107
19. Migration of Nephite People 113
20. Modern Topographical Map 120
21. Pyramid of Pacaritanpu 128
22. Diagram of the Pyramid of Ruins of Pacaritanpu 129
23. Cusco City Plan 142
24. Modern Map of Cusco 157
25. Schematic Drawing of Inca Trail 163
26. Cusco in the Form of a Puma 170
27. Map of Divided Incan Kingdom 172
28. Incan Southern Cross 182

29. Symbol of Incan Southern Cross 182
30. Map of Incan Empire 183
31. Map of Southern Cross 183
32. Combined Map of Incan Empire 183
33. Drawing of Temple of Koricancha 204
34. Drawing of Temple of Koricancha 231
35. Another Figure of the Temple of Koricancha 231
36. Map of underground tunnels in Cusco 234

ACKNOWLEDGEMENTS

First of all, this book is my own doing and responsibility. If there are any errors, they are my fault. I don't pretend to be a perfect scriptorian or even an expert on the subject of Pre-Columbian History, or even Book of Mormon Studies. I am, however, an avid reader and lifetime lover of the Book of Mormon. My sole interest in writing this book is to promote the Book of Mormon to the world and encourage more discussion and reading of this incredible volume of scripture.

I would also like to take this opportunity to sincerely thank all those individuals who have believed and helped on this project. I need to give a thank you to my children, especially my nephew Austin, and my sons Norman and Ryan, for their artistic skills in producing the maps, pictures, and illustrations. Austin designed the final manuscript with his illustrations and art work that gives this book a unique life of its own. Thanks I give to my wife, Christal, for her love and support through the years. My Heavenly Father has truly blessed me beyond measure. There have been many who have read and lent suggestions to the manuscript. I thank these people for their friendship and valuable contributions to the finished product. And last, a big thanks goes out to the publishers and marketers who wanted to publish a book written by one of the least in the Kingdom of God. Thank you…….L. (Les) Norman Shurtliff

DEDICATION

This book is dedicated to my mother, Edythe Jane, and my father, Norman Terry Shurtliff, who gave me life, and love. They were the first who taught me the gospel and instilled a desire within me to read and study the Book of Mormon. I have always felt like Nephi of old "I, Nephi, having been born of goodly parents,…" 1Nephi 1:1 How thankful I am to have been born of goodly parents like Nephi, and for their example and teachings to me. They have passed on now, but their legacy lives on in their children, grandchildren, and great-grandchildren. I love them forever, and this work is dedicated to them.

PREFACE

What prompts a poor country farm boy from Southern Nevada, transplanted to Canada, to write a book, any book? It isn't money or fame writing to a limited audience. It is really simply a love of the Book of Mormon and a people. As a young man, I had the opportunity as many did to go on a mission for the Church of Jesus Christ of Latter-Day Saints. My two year adventure took me to South America and Buenos Aires, Argentina. My first weeks and first experiences were spent on a bike; and trying to manipulate the old wreck on the dirt and cobble stone streets of that beautiful, choice land wasn't easy. This wasn't an ordinary bike of today's standard either, but an unwieldy, heavy, bi-ped of yesteryear. The bike was probably a model of the 1940's or 1950's. It had huge wide tires, not unlike the mountain bikes of today, but that is where the similarity ended. Anyway, in 1976, because of the cold war and general distrust of the U.S. and its leaders by the Argentines, there was an interesting theory that abounded about the LDS missionaries down there. Many Argentines actually believed that we were American spies sent down to South America to watch them. We, of course, were supposed to have ridden our old Argentine bikes 7000 miles from the continental U.S. to Argentina with all of our luggage strapped to our backs. My first week I was dead tired; just trying to keep up with my companion going only a few miles each day was a challenge. I could not imagine riding that old junky bike 7000 miles, through jungles and deserts back to the U.S., and still be alive. As absurd and funny as that sounds to us today; many of us harbour interesting theories as well about the Book of Mormon, that I am sure in time will seem just as crazy. In this book, I will present some of my own theories, opinions, and truths as I have come to know them. Some people will definitely find these things interesting or crazy, I'm sure; but it is what I believe about the Book of Mormon. Time and experience as a chemist has taught me that men's understanding is always changing. Truth, laws, and principles, however, are absolute and hopefully someday we will come to know the truth of all things. I will also present some theories, opinions, and facts that have come from other people's writing, and knowledge that are important to the purposes of this book. We all realize that truth comes from God and can only be discerned by His spirit. There will be some who will not agree with my opinions and theories, and that is fine with me. This book is just an attempt to present these opinions and theories to you, the reader; it is not my job to convince you of the truth of them.

Facing Picture for Chapter 1: Dramatized Composite Picture of Manco Capac, the First Inca as he overlooks his capitol city of Cusco, Peru. He was the Prophet Nephi from the Book of Mormon or in other words Nephi I.

CHAPTER 1

INTRODUCTION

This book begins with an introduction of what is hoped to be accomplished within its pages. Since the purpose of the gospel in these Latter Days is to 'Bring People Unto Christ' and the Book of Mormon is 'Another Testament of Jesus Christ', then our challenge is to build on these fundamental truths. To bring people closer to the truth and the gospel of Christ through the Book of Mormon is our quest. We hope to not detract from this mission but to enhance it and present evidence that the Book of Mormon is literally **true** in every sense of the word. In fact we believe that the Book of Mormon is the most correct book ever written. So, we will start with that premise and work backward if you will to collaborate the truth of the Book of Mormon. We are not trying to prove the Book of Mormon is true because we already know that, but what we are going to do is discover and find evidence and proof from the legends, geography, history, archaeology, and some physical attributes that establish the truth. We see the Book of Mormon as the absolute truth that all things are measured against in our study. We realize that much has been already written on this subject that is very compelling, however there is much more that must be written about this most important scriptural text. It is hoped that these discoveries are as wonderful for you, the reader, as they are for those that have already discovered them.

Truths

Truth is absolute and never changing. Truth comes from God to man through revelation to his chosen servants. We consider Joseph Smith to be the great 'Master Asker' in our dispensation. He wanted to know the truths associated with the scriptures and the Book of Mormon specifically and was privileged to have the Lord reveal many of these truths to him for our benefit in the latter days. Joseph Smith knew many things because of visitations from angels and other revelatory sources. Some of these truths have been written down and are well documented throughout the history of the church and other things are not so well known. He had a great desire to know, and now we are the beneficiaries of that quest for knowledge. In this book we will discuss at least two of those great truths that Joseph Smith learned regarding the Book of Mormon that are not well known in the Church today. The truth is that we know that the people and actual events of the Book of Mormon happened somewhere in the Americas, not just spiritually, but physically as well. The truth is that it all really did happen.

Legends

The legends of the native people are an important source of truth that can frequently help piece together the actual non-written history of its people. In this book we take a look at the South American legends of Wiracochan (Jesus Christ), Manco Capac (Nephi), and the Tree of Life. All of these legends have surprising similarities to accounts in the Book of Mormon. But, then again, how can they be surprising if they are true. All of these native traditions also point to the location of the City of Nephi being established at Cusco, Peru. There are also legends of other indigenous people that relate to the Book of Mormon in other lands, but none that we

{Picture Inside Ch #1} Ancient Inca record keeping to preserve the traditions, history and legends were done with a series of knotted strings woven into a necklace and called 'The Sacred Quipu'.

know about that so clearly establish the truth as presented in the Book of Mormon.

Travels of Nephi

It is critical to note that early Church Leaders knew and established the actual Lehi Landing in Chile which is paramount to our discussions. A bit of history and storyline is presented from the scriptures to establish exactly what Nephi writes regarding his travels. It is important to identify these concepts early so that they can provide a basis for further discussion about the location and characteristics of the People of Nephi and their cities and temples. Important traits and activities of this prophet leader are pointed out and discussed to help the reader more closely know this important character in the Book of Mormon and his role as a prophet leader.

Geography

We have taken a particularly different position based on the truths, legends, and other evidence we have compiled, to place the City of Nephi in Cusco, Peru. This book is a study of this city which is in the heart of South America and the center of Pre-Inca ruins. We will place the Book of Mormon lands in the Chile/Bolivia/Peru/Ecuador area instead of in Mexico and Central America as is common practice among the general church scholars of our day. We are not by any means original in this thought process, but it is still not the generally accepted concept on the matter. We hope to change that consensus with the compelling evidence that we and others will present here. In reality, the actual Book of Mormon story took place in a relatively small area, mostly in the Andean Highlands of South America. The two most important conceptual questions of the Book of Mormon geography to be discussed are: 1. Where did the Lehi landing in the New World occur? 2. Where is the narrow neck of land spoken of, that separated the land northward from the land southward?

Basic Theories

Theories about the archaeology of South America as compared to Mexico and Central America will be presented as well as theories about the migration of the Nephite peoples to the northern countries and Polynesia. Theories about Polynesia and their ancestry will be discussed. The actual geographical aspects of the Book of Mormon are theories that are important to this book. We will also present evidence that there are in fact two Hill Cumorahs, one in South America and the one in the State of New

York. If enough theories and circumstantial evidence collaborate a principle or truth then it can have a very good possibility or probability of it being a true principle.

Characteristics of the City of Nephi

We will enumerate various characteristics of the beautiful City of Nephi. This is the magnificent city that Nephi would have built and lived in most of his life. Much of this chapter is scriptural information that Nephi himself and others like wicked King Noah, presented for us as readers to teach us about his people and the blessings of God bestowed upon his people and this great city. Some of the characteristics of the City of Nephi would include: the temple as a central focal point of the city, towers, a fortress or refuge for protection, two sections of the city (an older and younger portion), secret passage ways, and a history of being the capital city of the Nephites and Lamanites for a thousand years, and so forth.

City of Cusco, Peru

Chapter Six identifies the City of Cusco, Peru, as the ancient City of Nephi, the Navel of the World, and the Center of the Universe. Nephi and his people were builders and industrious and left an everlasting legacy of their work behind for us to see and to appreciate today. Evidence from our time is presented that correlates with what is written and established in the scriptures and that coincides with this beautiful valley home of Nephi, which he established in the tops of the mountains, and a city which is Cusco, Peru. The 'Promised Land' that Nephi covenanted with the Lord to obtain. There are evidences from the city of Cusco which prove all of the characteristics that are spoken of in the Book of Mormon and can be compared to the descriptions from the scriptures.

Temple of Nephi

The temple that Nephi built was to follow after the manner of construction of the Temple of Solomon. Nephi's temple is clearly the focal point of our study. This structure is identified in scripture with all its attributes and references. It is purposely discussed as the most important structure of the capital city and of this incredible civilization. It was the focal point in the Center of Nephi's Universe, and of the city he and his people built, and a lasting legacy to the world of the evidence of this great civilization that Nephi established in the 'Promised Land'.

The Promise

In conclusion of this introductory chapter, we review a unique promise that comes from the ancient Lamanite prophet, Samuel, to the remnant of the Children of Lehi. At the time of this prophecy, the Lamanites were more righteous than the Nephites and because of their dedication and devotion they were given this promise:

> 10. And now, because of their steadfastness when they do believe in that thing which they do believe, for because of their firmness when they are once enlightened, behold, the Lord shall bless them and prolong their days, notwithstanding their iniquity—
>
> 11. Yea, even if they should dwindle in unbelief the Lord shall prolong their days, until the time shall come which hath been spoken of by our fathers, and also by the prophet Zenos, and many other prophets, concerning the restoration of our brethren, the Lamanites, again to the knowledge of the truth—
>
> 12. Yea, I say unto you, that in the latter times the promises of the Lord have been extended to our brethren, the Lamanites; and notwithstanding the many afflictions which they shall have, and notwithstanding they shall be driven to and fro upon the face of the earth, and be hunted, and shall be smitten and scattered abroad, having no place for refuge, the Lord shall be merciful unto them.
>
> 13. And this is according to the prophecy, that they shall again be brought to the true knowledge, which is the knowledge of their Redeemer, and their great and true shepherd, and be numbered among his sheep.
>
> Helaman 15:10-13

This great prophecy says that once again these people will be favored of the Lord and come to a knowledge of the truth of the gospel and will embrace it. With that knowledge of truth in the latter days will come a realization of who they are, where they came from, where they lived, and who they will become. And just like the Lamanites in earlier times, these Children of Lehi will again discover their heritage and discard the false teachings of their fore fathers. In the past forty years the Church has gone from no temples in South America to one in every nation; with many countries having multiple temples. The growth of the Church in South America has increased dramatically as the Lord's covenant people are learning who they are and coming unto Christ in great numbers. It is a fulfillment of this prophecy of Samuel, and it is indeed proof of the veracity of this great work. The Children of Lehi will come to a knowledge of their Savior and be numbered in His Church. This prophecy is literally true and is now coming about, and it is the purpose of this book to bring these truths from the Book of Mormon to this chosen people, and to bring people to Christ. There is currently a 'Marvellous Work and a Wonder' happening amongst this people. A marvellous miracle is occurring with the Lord's children specifically in South America. The sole purpose of this book is to increase faith and testimony among all true believers in Jesus Christ and this other testament, the Book of Mormon.

Facing Picture Ch#2: The famous ruins of Machu Pichu that were discovered by Hiram Bingham. One of the most beautiful vistas in all the world. One of the great tourist attractions of Peru.

CHAPTER 2

TRUTHS

Truth is the fundamental foundation that we need to start with in our study of the Book of Mormon. There are so many theories and suppositions out there, that it is nice to start on a firm foundation for all of us. There have been many scholars and teachers that have postulated their positions regarding the geography of the Book of Mormon. Those theories take us to Central America, the Yucatan, and even to North America. In the end there seems to be much confusion amongst the scholars of the Church in our day regarding the geography of the Book of Mormon. The reality for most people is that the common consensus of opinion is that Lehi and his family traveled in the desert around the Arabian Peninsula to Oman and the Land Bountiful. There they built a ship and traveled to the New World and their 'Promised Land'. The Book of Mormon documents this 2500 mile eight-year travail in the wilderness and deserts of Arabia very well and we are generally together geographically speaking until they embark on their oceanic journey. Here then is where the problem really arises. **Where did Lehi's party land in the New World?** If we can really substantiate this great question, then it solves for the students of the Book of Mormon most of the problems with regard to the geography of this sacred scripture.

Why is this important? Some may ask why do we even care about the geography? Shouldn't the doctrine be the most important thing? Who cares about where it happened? Isn't the Book of Mormon a volume of scripture, and shouldn't it be just a spiritual issue and not one of physical nature? The interesting fact here is that there is room in our testimonies for physical confirmation as well as spiritual confirmation. Actually, we many times can feel physically the spirit working in our lives. So, both can work together and actually do in everything we undertake. The wonderful thing is that Joseph Smith also had this same question come to his mind and asked the Lord for an answer. So, it must have been important for us to know if the Prophet Joseph wanted to know and if the Lord decided it was important enough to give him an answer to the question. We believe that in the early days of the Church, Joseph Smith actually taught the principle or truth of where the Lehi colony landed. Fredrick G. Williams was the prophet's scribe and a counsellor in the presidency. In his handwriting Williams writes down presumably from the lips of the prophet this important truth. Whether it was at the time of the receiving of the seventh section of the Doctrine and Covenants (April 1829) or later during the Kirtland era during the School of the Prophets (April to August 1832) it does not matter. The truth and information was most assuredly given to the prophet himself through revelation and written down by his faithful scribe. It must be an important truth where Lehi's colony landed to have been preserved down to the present day in the Church Archives. The following page is a scan of the actual preserved document from the Church Archives that brings to light the answer to prayerful questions through divine revelation to the Prophet Joseph Smith. This source document becomes the cornerstone for truth that establishes the geography of the Book of Mormon. It will provide the framework for the rest of the discussion in this manuscript because it gives us a solid fundamental starting point in the New World. This starting point establishes where to begin our quest for truth.

Document #1: Source Document for the 'Lehi Landing' from Church Archives handwritten by Fredrick G. Williams, scribe to the Prophet. It could have been given through the Urim and Thumin to Joseph Smith and Oliver Cowdery in April 1829 or during the School of the Prophets during the Kirtland era, (April to August 1832).

A revelation concerning John the beloved disciple

Now the Lord said unto me John my beloved, what desirest thou? And I said Lord give unto me power that I may bring souls unto thee, and the Lord said unto me verily I say unto thee because thou desirest this, thou shalt tarry till I come in my glory, and for this cause the Lord said unto Peter, if I will that he tarry till I come, what is that to thee for he desired of me that he might bring souls unto me, but thou desirest that thou might speedily come unto me in my kingdom. I say unto thee Peter this was a good desire, But my beloved hath undertaken a greater work; verily I say unto you ye shall both have according to your desires for ye both have joy in that which ye have desired &c &c &c ——

Question asked in English & answers in hebrew

For it grieveth me that I should lose this tree & the fruit thereof

Ans: ofin Bemin esmon E, Zee oms ifs veris itzer ensuens vineris ——

English Brethren bid you adieu

Ans: Efs E' Zamti'

Characters on the book of Mormon

(The book of Mormon)   The interpreters of languages

L. Cp   O₁₁   C₁₁

The course that Lehi travelled from the city of Jerusalem to the place where he and his family took ships, they travelled nearly a south south east direction untill they come to the nineteenth degree of North Latitude, then nearly east to the sea of Arabia then sailed in a south east direction and landed on the continent of South America in Chili thirty degrees South Latitude ———

This handwritten paper is the source document for the 'Lehi Landing' and it contains part of section seven in our Doctrine and Covenants. The middle section contains some Hebrew words and then their English translation. Also, some ancient characters from the Book of Mormon translation are written down here. This part of the document has prompted some church historians to speculate that Frederic G. Williams was merely writing down notes from the prophet during a session of the School of the Prophets in Kirtland in 1832. You will notice at the bottom of the page the final paragraph wherein the landing place of the family of Lehi in the Promised Land is revealed. The paragraph says the following:

> "The course that Lehi traveled from the city of Jerusalem to the place where he and his family took ship, they traveled nearly a south southeast direction until they came to the nineteenth degree of north latitude, then nearly east to the sea of Arabia then sailed in a south east direction and landed on the continent of South America in Chile thirty degrees South Latitude."

An analysis of this important document from the archives is warranted here. Why is section seven involved? Section seven is important Latter-Day Saint doctrine. The section talks about John the Beloved, one of the Savior's apostles and his desire to stay on the earth and bring souls unto Christ. Why would a comment about Lehi's Landing be on the same document as this revelation about John is a fair question to ask? They seem like two completely different subjects. The prophet Joseph Smith with the use of the interpreters and with his scribe Oliver Cowdery translated The Book of Mormon in approximately twelve weeks from April to June of 1829. Joseph Smith asked the Lord in prayer many questions during the process of the translation which were answered in the form of direct revelation by means of the Urin and Thumin, Seer Stone, and other means. These revelations were written down at a later time by Frederick G. Williams, the prophet's scribe, as they flowed from the prophet's own mouth. Presumably, they are connected because the prophet probably had been translating the portion of Third Nephi where it talks about the three Nephites and their desire to stay on the earth and bring souls unto Christ. This would have been an answer to his question about John the Beloved and if he had had the same gift granted unto him. The prophet's scribe merely records on the same piece of paper the answer to another question that Joseph had received by divine revelation regarding the landing of Lehi and his family in the Americas. There is really nothing odd or speculative about this document. The two doctrines were both answers to questions and the prayers of the Prophet Joseph Smith.

This revelation though is not widely taught in the church as a whole. It should be not only taught but also sounded by trumpet loud and clear for all to hear. **Lehi landed in Chile on the Thirtieth Parallel on the Western coast of South America.** This is the first great truth that is the foundation for this book that celebrates the life of the Prophet Nephi and the city that he built. In Chapter 5, Book of Mormon Geography, other quotes from early church leaders and scholars on the 'Lehi Landing' will be discussed that broaden and substantiate this truth and point to this early document as being the source document for later teachings after the death of the prophet Joseph Smith.

The second great truth is actually derived from the first and that is: **Nephi built his city and lived all of his days in South America.** The Book of Mormon language and text does not allow Nephi an option of traveling more than a thousand miles from the landing site or getting on a ship to go somewhere else. The Book of Mormon clearly says:

"… and did journey in the wilderness for the space of many days." 2Nephi 5:7

So, after Nephi's party traveled 'many days' in the wilderness then they pitched their tents and called the place the Land of Nephi. Here Nephi built his city and a temple to God, and here the Nephites lived for the next 450 years (from about 590 B.C. to 140 B.C.). We will define the term 'many days' and discuss these points in greater detail in future chapters. Therefore, we have actually established two truths regarding the Book of Mormon that can be the solid foundation for more study and discussion that has resulted in this work, *The City of Nephi*. Until we have more divine revelation to our modern day prophets from God then much of the rest of this information will remain legends, theories, and suppositions. At least now we do not have Lehi's family stranded on the shores of the 'Land Bountiful'. We have actually landed them in the 'Promised Land' and specifically to the western shores of northern Chile. From here we can launch into the unknown and speculate what physically happened in the Book of Mormon account.

TWO IMPORTANT TRUTHS

1. Lehi's family landed in Chile on the Thirtieth Parallel on the Western coast South America.

2. Nephi built his city and lived all of his days in South America.

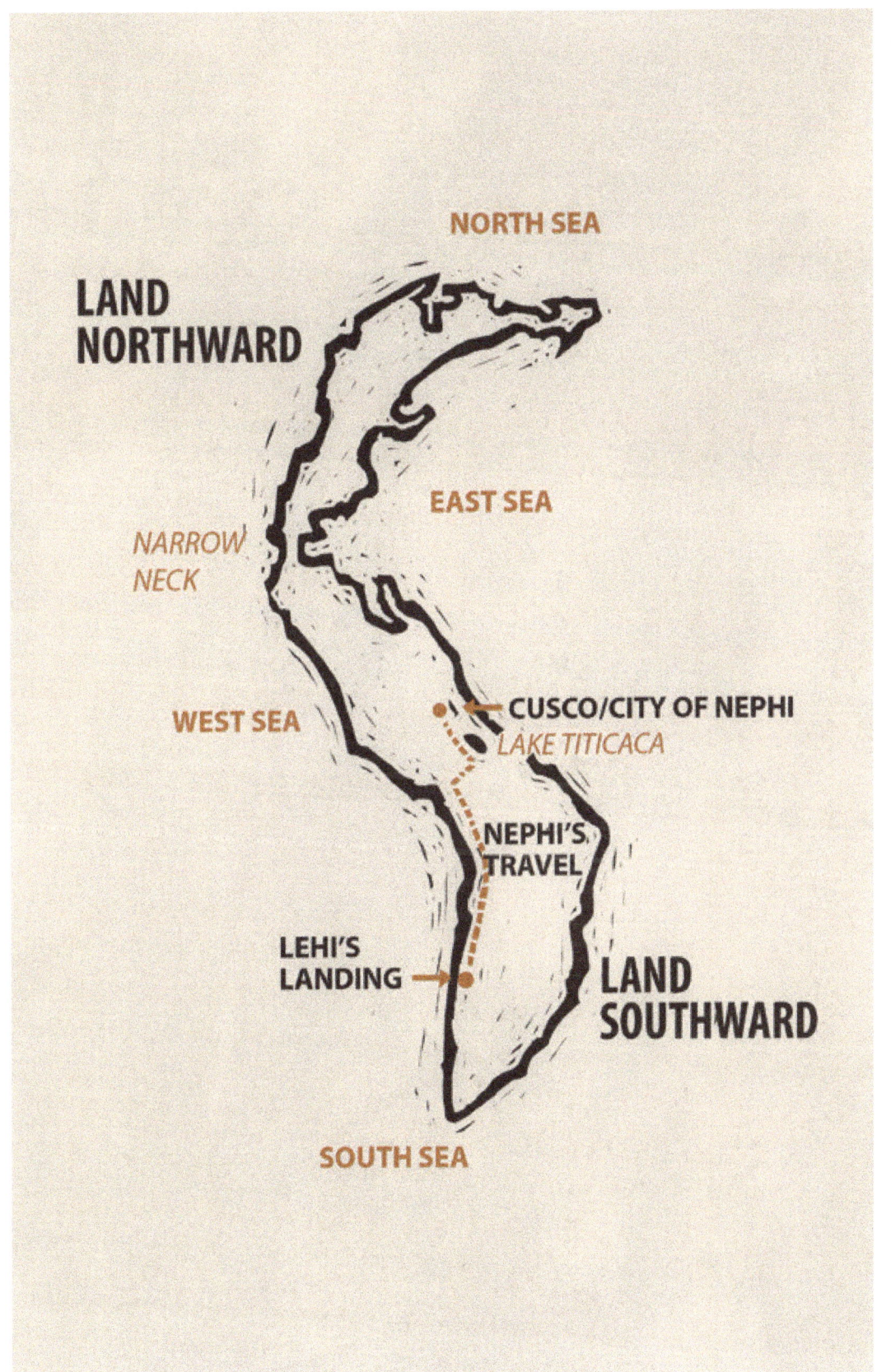

Introduction Map #1
This is a map of South America showing where Lehi's colony landed and then Nephi's subsequent escape into the wilderness for 'Many Days'. The dotted line shows the probable course of his journey to the City of Nephi (Cusco, Peru).

THE CITY OF NEPHI

{Facing Picture for Ch #3} The ancient inhabitants of Ollaytaytambo carved the face of Wiracochan (Jesus Christ) on their mountain, 'To Always Remember Him'.

CHAPTER 3

LEGENDS

This chapter focuses on South America and the Pre-Inca people of the Andean Highlands. Many of the myths and legends were written down by the 'rememberers', the early Spanish Chroniclers, during the 16th century and the Inquisition Period. These legends are not new and have been talked about for the nearly five centuries since Pizarro. There are several legends of note with the Inca and Pre-Inca peoples that correspond directly with Book of Mormon teachings. These legends so closely tie in to the accounts of Nephi and his followers, as well as the coming of Christ to the Americas that it is completely amazing. The legends of an indigenous people are very interesting because there can be quite a bit of truth and history that has been handed down for generations contained in them. Obviously, some parts or concepts will become corrupted or embellished during the process of telling and retelling the stories over time. We can, however, remarkably match up some of these legends from the ancient peoples with the religious history from the Book of Mormon that we know to be true.

Wiracochan and the Sacred Path

The Legend of Wiracocha is the first one that we will review, and a good place to start. One of the best descriptions of the Legend of

Wiracocha (Our Heavenly Father) and Wiracochan (Jesus Christ) is found in an account "The Sacred Valley of the Incas" by Fernando and Edgar Salazar. Reference #1, Chapter Note #1

> "......They say that in the beginning, before the reign of the Inca, Wiracocha created a dark world and after ordering the heavens and the earth, he created a race of giants. He commanded them to live in peace, to serve him and when they did not obey him, he changed them into stones and at the same time sent a great flood named Unu Pachacuti which means 'the-water-which-transformed-the-world.'"

An interesting fact is that many of these ancient legends contain references to stories from the Old Testament such as: Adam and Eve and the creation, the Tree of Life, the flood, the tower to get to heaven, Moses and the parting of the Red Sea, looking upon serpents (Jesus Christ) to be healed, and the fiery flying serpents. All of these stories were immortalized in their lives through the telling of these stories to their children and in their architectural construction. The people of the world today find these stories incredulous because they believe these indigenous people supposedly had no bible or written language, and also that they came across the Bering Strait and descended from the cave men of Asia. We know from the Book of Mormon of course that Lehi's family were able to bring with them to the 'Promised Land' the Brass Plates which contained at least the first five books of Moses from the Bible. In this first account we find mentioned a reference to the creation and the flood. The legend continues:

> "When the rains passed and the earth dried, Wiracocha decided to populate it for a second time and, to do so more perfectly, he determined to create lamps that would give light; for that purpose, he went to the great lake Titicaca and there he commanded the Sun and the Moon and the Stars to come out of the lake and rise into the heavens in order to give light to the world. And they say that the Moon was brighter than the Sun, and for that reason, just at the moment when they arose into the sky, the Sun threw a fistful of ashes into the Moon's face, and from that moment the Moon has stayed the color it is now.

Picture #1 Wiracochan's image carved on the face of Mt. Pinkuylluna to remind the native inhabitants of the Son of God's visit to the Sacred Valley.

> And after all this had happened, from out of the South appeared the messenger of Wiracocha, who was a man with a big body and his face showed that he was a personage of great authority and was called Wiracochan or Tunupa. He dressed in a tattered tunic that reached to his feet; his hair was short and had a crown on his head and carried a staff like those priest and astronomers of old. They also say that he carried on his shoulder a sack full of gifts which he gave to the people who listened to him. And they say that this man had great powers such that he could make the mountains become plains and cause the plains to become mountains. And he did other greater things as well, because he gave life to men and animals, and from his hand flowed great benefits."

The character of Wiracochan in this legend of course is Jesus Christ who appeared to the Nephites in 34A.D. He taught the people, healed their sick and blessed them. Christ appeared among the people and wrought many mighty miracles, and then ascended up into heaven in a marvellous way. The legend continues:

> "Then he went to Tiahuanaco and there he drew and sculpted upon a huge slab all the nations that he planned to create and nourish, and after that he began his pilgrimage, performing miracles along the way as he traveled the mountainous paths, ordering the peoples to come out from their Paqarinas, saying: 'Peoples and Nations, listen and obey, for I order you to come out and multiply and fill the earth,' and at his voice all the places obeyed and so some of the peoples came out of the earth and others from the lakes, springs, valleys, caves, trees, cliffs, and shrubs. And he designed for each village the costume and clothes each should wear, and in the same fashion he gave to each nation the language each should speak, along with their songs and seeds. And, thus, as he wandered along his way through the Andes and the mountains of the earth, he went on giving out names to all the trees, great and small, as well as the flowers and fruits, showing to the people those which were good to eat and those which were good for medicine, and in the same way did he give names to the herbs and grasses and showed when they were to flower and bear fruit. He also instructed the men how to live, speaking to them lovingly with great mildness, admonishing them to be good,

telling them not to hurt one another nor do one another damage; later, he taught them to cultivate the earth; he broke the ground with the point of his staff so that it was ready to plant and, thus, with only a word from him, he made the corn and other plants grow....

....This Wiracochan, whom the people also called Tunupa,.... which means Messenger of Wiracocha, his fountain, the preacher, he-who-is-in-charge-of-the-present, and the-knower-of-time, went to the town of the curaca Apotambo (Lord of Tanpu, Tambo or Ollantaytambo). When he arrived, they were celebrating a marriage ceremony. It was in these circumstances that of understanding and love, but the people of the town would not hear him. He reprimanded them for this in loving tones and then, in a gesture of reciprocity, he gave the staff he carried, upon which was engraved all his knowledge, to the curaca Apotambo. After that, in memory of Wiracochan, they laboured to carve a mountain in his image and they venerated it greatly.

Afterwards, this Wiracochan continued on his way still doing his marvellous works and finally arrived at the line where the day is as long as the night, near the Equator, where, desiring to leave the earth, he told them that in time, there would come some men who would claim to be Wiracochas and that they were not to be believed. And they say that then he went into the sea, walking upon the water as if he were foam..."

It is incredible to note here that when Francisco Pizarro arrived on the shores of Peru for the first time in 1528 the superstitious natives heralded Pizarro as this God, Wiracochan, that promised would return someday. It helped Pizarro's status that he came by sea floating on the foam or surf into the Bay of Tumbes just like the prophecy predicted in the narrow neck of land. Prince Atahualpa could have easily swept the small group of Spaniards (little more than 200 soldiers) off the land at the battle of Cajamarca five years later in 1532 except for these prophesied legends.

"It is said that after time passed, and as the town of Tambo or Ollantaytambo flourished, thanks to the knowledge given to the people by Wiracochan, the staff he had left transformed itself into fine gold at the very moment of the birth of one of

THE CITY OF NEPHI 33

the descendants, of Apotambo, Manco Capac, who later became the first Inca. After some years had passed, he took the golden staff and went up into the high mountain ranges and there found the place which came to be the capital of the Empire of the Incas: Cusco." Ref #1. The Sacred Valley of the Incas Myths and Symbols, Fernando E. Elorrieta Salazar and Edgar Elorrieta Salazar.

On a subsequent page is a picture of the face of Wiracochan or Tunupa sculpted on the side of the mountain, Pinkuylluna, and also an artist's rendition of the figure of Wiracochan. It is drawn to show the bearded fair skinned man carrying his bundle of gifts for the people that he carried with him as he traveled from place to place teaching the people, healing them,

Picture #2
This is a statue of Francisco Pizarro who conquered Cusco, the Incan capital, on November 15th 1533. It is found today in the capital city he built Lima, Peru.

and doing other mighty miracles. A note of interest here is that the beard is significant because the ancient peoples of this area had very little or no facial hair at all, and also Wiracochan was fair skinned. Wiracochan came at a time when there were many earthquakes, lightnings, and thunderings. He taught the people to love each other and not make war any more. And he promised that he would someday return, leaving by walking out onto the foam and waves of the sea and into the clouds. It therefore was not hard to imagine why the Inca Prince, Atahualpa, knowing of the ancient prophecy did not protect himself sufficiently against the invasion of Pizarro and his conquistadores. In 1532 this bearded white-man, Francisco Pizarro, and his 63 horseman and 200 infantrymen arrived on the coasts of Peru in their white masted sailing ships, riding upon the foam of the sea. They carried with them their cannon and blunderbuss or harquebus which provided ample thunder and lightening for the superstitious Incas. Atahualpa (commanding an army of perhaps 200,000 warriors) thinking Pizarro came in peace and love, granted an audience and a meeting to the conquistador who promptly captured him in a flurry of gunfire and confusion. Then later, the Spaniards executed the Inca Prince anyway, even after exacting a huge ransom of one room filled with gold and two rooms of silver from the native people of the Northern Kingdom.

The prophecies of the ancient Incan people foretold of Wiracochan returning one day to establish a new kingdom of peace forever. Atahualpa was so convinced that Pizarro was indeed this white bearded god of their ancestral traditions that he did not even arm his warriors in their monumental meeting in the main square of the city of Cajamarca on November 15th 1532. On that fateful day, the first physical contact with the Europeans was a Franciscan Friar presenting Atahualpa with a copy of the Bible stating that they had come in the name of Christ with His Word. Atahualpa placed the Bible to his ear, and hearing nothing threw it to the ground in disgust. It was an act of heresy to the conquistadors, and Francisco Pizarro gave out the infamous shout, "Santiago" (St. James). It was the signal for his little army to commence their attack or massacre. The Bible of all things was the sign and signal of this brutal conquest. A paradox of incredible proportions is that Pizarro conquered Peru and the Incan Empire by force in the name of Christianity, even though the kingdom was generously given to him freely by a people who generally believed that he was this loving Son of God, Wiracochan, or the Messenger of Wiracocha.

A student of the Book of Mormon readily recognizes the similarities between the Legend of Wiracochan and our Savior, Jesus Christ, who in the midst of an era of tremendous earthquakes and volcano eruptions visited

Lehi's Promised Land and its inhabitants. We can visualize the Savior walking these ancient lands, teaching and healing the people as he visited them. He went about the people giving them gifts, spiritual and physical as he traveled among them. This is part of our understanding of the scriptures, and it is also the history of this chosen people and a time honored legend from ancient times.

Legend of Wiracochan

In the Sacred Valley, the valley of the Urubamba River, just 20 Km away from Cusco is where the beautifully hand carved face of Wiracochan is seen on the mountain side of Pinkuylluna, next to the city of Ollantaytambo. The sacred or holy mountain, Pinkuylluna, itself is a type of ancient solar calendar that the priests or astronomers used to tell the day of the year by the sun's position at daybreak on the crest of the mountain. These pivotal points where the sun was 'tied' seem to be the axis around which the sun moves in the course of a year.

Ollantaytambo is an ancient city or way station on the Inca road to Machu Pichu, designed anciently in the shape of a cob of corn, or their 'Staff of Life' where all life originated. Wiracochan or Viracochan is the name of the Son of God, who came to teach these people anciently. Wiracochan (Jesus Christ) was the messenger of Wiracocha (God). Viracochan (Wiracochan sometimes is spelled with a 'V') was a bearded white God who visited amongst the people. He taught them to love each other and many other things. He healed the sick, and raised the dead. He traveled from village to village with a bundle of gifts on his back. Incredibly, this legend corresponds exactly to the coming of Christ to the Americas, where he taught his people, established His church, and did many miracles. See Figure #1… This picture shows the crown and face of Wiracochan carved into the mountain, with his sack of gifts upon his back for the people.

The crown or hat, "Chuku", on top of his head designates the office of an Inca High Priest. The chronicler Blas Valera in 1590 wrote: "The Inca priest was a personage respected by all the great lords and the people. He observed much abstinence in his manner of living as he never ate meat but only herbs and roots accompanied by corn bread; he did not drink wine but only took water, his home was in the countryside, not in populated places; he rarely spoke and he dressed in a simple wool garment which reached to his knees and on top he wore a drab cloak of black and purple. His life in

Picture #3
The sacred Mount Pinkuylluna is 'tied' to the sun.

the countryside allowed him to contemplate and meditate more freely upon the stars and the other things of his religion…" Ref 2.

On the solstice of each year, when the sunlight shines through the mountains on the opposite side of the valley it lights up the top of the head, the crown or consciousness of Wiracochan. Each day between the hour of 2:30 and 3:30 in the afternoon Wiracochan's eyes come out of the shadows and are lit up by the sun's rays and he "awakens". This is one way the ancient people were able to symbolically show that Wiracochan "sees" and "knows" them personally. It was designed…"so that not only is he present among us, but also to show us his continued vigilance. It is for this, each day he 'wakes up'." Ref 1.

What a great way to remember our Savior, Jesus Christ, by carving His face upon the mountain. Knowing that He sees us and knows us personally and is always conscious of our needs each day is a good way to demonstrate to the ancient Nephites and Lamanites of His love for each of us. They immortalized this concept for centuries by carving His countenance upon

Figure #1 Artist's representation of Wiracochan on Mount Pinkuylluna.

the side of Mount Pinkuylluna. The ancient Nephites did not each have a set of scriptures on scrolls or plates and most probably could not even read their own language. So, how better to remember and review the teachings of their leaders and the prophets than to observe these concepts daily in their mountainous surroundings. Therefore, it would be fulfilling the commandment 'To Always Remember Him'.

Legend of Manco Capac

The legend of the first Inca, Manco Capac, is an amazing similarity to Nephi and the early Nephites from the Book of Mormon. The rememberers down through the centuries have taught the story of Manco Capac, and his wife, Mama Capac. God brought Manco Capac up out of the blue crystal clear waters of Lake Titicaca where all life began. Manco Capac with his wife, Mama Capac, lived in a cave near the waters of the beautiful lake where they nurtured their family. God spoke to Manco Capac and told him to go forth and find a new land and gave him a golden staff. Where upon he was to put forth his staff and when it sank into the ground that would be the place where they would build their city. Manco Capac traveled from Lake Titicaca north with his family which consisted of his wife and children and his sisters, and three brothers and their sister wives and children. On their journey they paused for a while in the Sacred Valley and founded Ollantaytambo. The legend says that when Manco Capac arrived in the Cuzco Valley he did thrust in his golden staff into the ground and it sank down deep and quickly disappeared. The sign had been given and Manco Capac knew his wanderings were over. Ref 3. We can almost hear him declare, "This is where we will stay and build our city and our temple to God." The City of Nephi with its Nephite culture took root and started to grow. It would become the Nephite capitol for the next 450 years.

The legend so closely parallels the Book of Mormon story of Nephi and his three brothers that it is incredible and gives one almost an eerie

Pictures #4 & 5
Wiracochan wakes up as the sun hits his face every afternoon.

feeling. Of course, Nephi was warned by the Lord to depart into the wilderness, and take those souls with him who wanted to go. They took with them the liahona or ball of curious workmanship that God had prepared to direct them in their travels in the wilderness. Nephi also carried with him the Brass Plates, and the Sword of Laban which was made of precious steel and a golden hilt, (the golden staff in the Incan legend).

> 9. "And I beheld his sword, and I drew it forth from the sheath thereof; and the hilt thereof was of pure gold, and the workmanship thereof was exceedingly fine, and I saw that the blade thereof was of the most precious steel." (1 Nephi 4:9)

> 12. "And I, Nephi, had also brought the records which were engraven upon the plates of brass; and also the ball, or compass, which was prepared for my father by the hand of the Lord, according to that which is written....

> 14. And I, Nephi, did take the sword of Laban, and after the manner of it did make many swords...." (1Nephi 5:12, 14)

It does not require much imagination to see in your mind, this prophet, Nephi, in search of a new 'Promised Land' being directed by the Liahona and testing the soil depth with his sword as he went. When he got

THE CITY OF NEPHI 39

to the beautiful valley of Cuzco and tested the rich soil, his golden sword sank deep into the ground. Here he said, "This is the place where we will build our city and a temple to our God." Nephi and Sam were married to the daughters of Ishmael. Zoram, the servant of Laban, also married a daughter of Ishmael as well. (1Nephi 16:7) Nephi's younger brothers, Jacob and Joseph, were probably also later married to either younger daughters of Ishmael, or other family members. So, in accordance with the Legend of Manco Capac, Nephi and his brothers then being married to daughters of Ishmael, would make their wives literally all 'sister wives'. Also, the Book of Mormon speaks of Nephi's presumably younger sisters that went with them into the wilderness (1Nephi 5:6).

Garcilaso de la Vega, (Ref 3.) a Spanish chronicler, whose father was a conquistador and his mother an Inca princess, wrote that Manco Capac and his sister-wife (Mama Capac), between them, taught the people the arts and industries; he instructed the men in agriculture and introduced the laws of the society, she taught the women to spin and weave. Ref 3. Garcilaso de la Vega, The Incas, 1539-1616 translated by Maria Jolas.

A person can compare the legend of Manco Capac with what the Book of Mormon says about the prophet Nephi and his followers in the passage below:

> "And we did observe to keep the judgments and the statutes, and the commandments of the Lord in all things, according to the Law of Moses.
>
> And the Lord was with us; and we did prosper exceedingly; for we did sow seed, and we did reap again in abundance. And we began to raise flocks, and herds, and animals of every kind.
>
> And I did teach my people to build buildings, and to work in all manner of wood, and of iron, and of copper, and of brass, and of steel, and of gold, and of silver, and of precious ores, which were in great abundance.
>
> And it came to pass that I, Nephi, did cause my people to be industrious, and to labor with their hands." 2Nephi 5:10-11, 15 & 17.

Bertrand Flornoy in *World of the Incas* is quoted as follows: "Manco Capac, it is said was pale-faced or white." Ref 4. **Manco Capac, the**

Picture #6 Beautiful colors have always been a characteristic of Peruvian textiles.

founder of Cusco, then was a pale-faced, white explorer married to a sister-wife of his three brothers' wives who came from the south looking for a new land with his family. What other legends by the indigenous American races could be more precise and more closely follow the life of Nephi and his family. Here you have a 'white, pale-faced' man taking his brothers and their 'sister-wives' north into the wilderness while searching for a new land to colonize. And he used a golden staff (Sword of Laban) to test the soil depth as they went.

The name Manco Capac means 'royal master' or 'chief', and the chronicler Santacruz Pachacuti (1613) referred to Manco Capac as the first Inca or king. Ref 5. This is very interesting because the Book of Mormon refers to Nephi as the first king, and then that the kingdom was handed down from father to son for many generations, each in turn being named as King Nephi II, King Nephi III, and so on. Jacob says about Nephi and the kings the following:

> "Wherefore, the people were desirous to retain in remembrance his name. And whoso should reign in his stead were called by the people, second Nephi, third Nephi, and so forth, according to the reigns of the kings; and thus they were called by the people, let them be of whatever name they would." Jacob 1:11

It is no wonder that for many centuries during the reign of the Incan Empire, the Inca king was designated the same way as in the Book of Mormon using the title of Inca I, Inca II, Inca III, and so on. Upon the arrival of Pizarro to Peru, the reigning monarch was Inca XI or Huayna Capac; which was the eleventh king in the Incan Dynasty.

Three Sacred Articles
The Myth of the Ayar Brothers

Another version of the same Legend of Manco Capac is presented here because of the importance of the prophet Nephi to our study of the Book of Mormon and it also brings out some other interesting concepts important to later theories that will be covered. The Myth of the Ayar Brothers is then another version of the Legend of Manco Capac.

> "And in the moment the Sun rose into the sky, Wiracocha appeared in the form of a splendid man and created the Incas. Then, from among them, he called the most important, the

eldest, named Manco Capac, and he said to him: 'You and your descendants will be great lords and will subject many nations; you should revere me always as a father, and, as my sons, you will always be respected.' After this, he gave them as insignia the Sunturpaucar, the Chanpi and the Tupayauri, and he bid them wander where they would, and wherever they would rest, he told them to try to thrust the Tupayauri in the soil. (This was an instrument in the form of a golden staff) and, where it should sink into the earth, there they should found a great city." Ref 1 p.39.

The three sacred articles that were given to Manco Capac by Wiracocha were the Sunturpaucar, the Chanpi, and the Tupayauri (golden staff or sword). Correspondingly, there are three sacred articles that the Lord gave Nephi; who took with him into the wilderness that became a cause of contention between the Lamanites and the Nephites for the next thousand years. The descendants of Laman and Lemuel would claim that Nephi stole them and robbed the Lamanites of these precious items. These were of course the Brass Plates, the Liahona, and the Sword of Laban; all were sacred gifts from God. In Mosiah it talks about the eternal hatred of the Lamanites towards the Nephites and that they taught their children also to hate the Nephites for stealing and taking the Brass Plates with them.

> "And again, they were wroth with him because he departed into the wilderness as the Lord had commanded him, and took the records which were engraven on the plates of brass, for they said that he robbed them.
> And thus they have taught their children that they should hate them, and that they should murder them, and that they should rob and plunder them, and do all they could to destroy them; therefore they have an eternal hatred towards the children of Nephi." Mosiah 10:16-17.

Nephi refers to these three sacred articles and taking them with him into the wilderness and simply states in the Book of Mormon that they did journey in the wilderness for the space of 'many days' and then they pitched their tents in a place which they called 'Nephi' (2Nephi 5:5-8). Then the prophet Nephi states the following in verse 12:

> "And I, Nephi had also brought the records which were engraven upon the plates of brass; and also the ball, or compass,

which was prepared for my father by the hand of the Lord, according to that which is written." 2Nephi 5:12

In verse 14 he mentions that he took the sword of Laban and made many other swords like it to defend themselves against the Lamanites, because of their hatred towards them. It is very clear that these same three sacred articles from the Book of Mormon are also the same three articles or possessions that Manco Capac carried with him to Cusco.

The Three Sacred Possessions

Book of Mormon Name	Incan Name	Description of Article
Brass Plates	Sunturpaucar	Scriptures-First Five Books of Moses
Liahona	Chanpi	Ball of Directors or Compass
Sword of Laban	Tupayauri	Golden staff – Gold hilted sword

The Children of the Sun
The account of the Ayar Brothers continues:

> "Thus, they came out of Titicaca and traveled north trying to stick the Tupayauri into the ground in all the places they passed until they came to a beautiful valley, and following the river Vilcanota or Willcamayu (Sacred River) which flowed through it, they rested at Tanpu or Tambo. There, they entered into the basements of a beautiful edifice called Pacaritanpu which means House of Dawn or House of Windows….The old men, the Quipucamayoc, who were the official historians of the Inca, recount how, at dawn one day, the earth of the Pacaritanpu opened in a place called Tanputtoco or Capacttoco (which is a construction in the shape of a window directed towards the earth) and, at that precise moment, Manco Capac, or Ayar Manco, was engendered by a Sun ray ….afterwards his brothers also came out, and they were called Ayar Cachi, Ayar Aucca and Ayar Uchu accompanied by their women named Mama Ocllo, Mama Cura, Mama Ragua, and Mama Huaco, all of them dressed very richly in costumes of wool and gold….The men carried staves of gold

and the women carried the service with which they would attend their husbands, and also seeds and foods. At once, they had come out into the world they walked about, turning as they walked so the light of the Sun sparkled on them and for all these reasons, they were called the Children of the Sun. After this marvellous occurrence, they again took up their long march." Ref 1. p.39-41

The obvious connection between the 'Children of the Sun' walking in the light of Wiracocha needs be made between the people of Manco Capac and the followers of Nephi. The obedience of Nephi's people to God and His commandments endowed these people from on high and made them a covenant people of the Lord. The light of truth and knowledge was in them. They glowed with the power of God and would have been described symbolically the same as the 'Children of Sun' or as we express it, the Children of God.

The Mystery of Sam – Nephi's Older Brother
The Legend of Ayar Cachi

Whatever happened to Sam, Nephi's brother, and why does he not play a more dominant role in the Book of Mormon? When Lehi blessed Sam he said:

> "11. And after he had made an end of speaking unto them, he spake unto Sam, saying: Blessed art thou, and thy seed; for thou shalt inherit the land like unto thy brother, and thy seed like unto his seed; and thou shalt be blessed in all thy days." 2Nephi 4:11

The blessing to Sam and his posterity was different than any other of Lehi's progeny.

Every serious student of the Book of Mormon has probably wondered about the character of Sam, Nephi's older brother. Could he have died by an accident or sickness on the way to the City of Nephi? Nephi took Sam and his family with him to this new land.

> "Wherefore, it came to pass that I, Nephi, did take my family, and also Zoram and his family, and Sam, mine elder brother and his family, and Jacob and Joseph, my younger brethren, and also my sisters, and all those who would go with me…." 1Nephi 5:6.

The name of Sam is never mentioned again in the plates which is extremely noteworthy. Even Jacob after announcing the death of Nephi said, "Now the people which were not Lamanites were Nephites; nevertheless, they were called Nephites, Jacobites, Josephites, Zoramites, Lamanites, Lemuelites, and Ishmaelites." Jacob 1:13. All the male patriarchs of Lehi's original group are mentioned here except Sam. This would indicate that either all of Sam's posterity were female or that the male side of this tribe died out at an early stage. And very possibly Sam could have met an untimely death at an early age as the following legend suggests with the death of Ayar Cachi. The personalities of Sam and Zoram are also curious to us as Book of Mormon readers because they were apparently very faithful and loyal to Nephi and to the Lord. However, they did not intervene or help Nephi in his struggles against his older brothers. But, the record is clear that they both followed him into the wilderness and became part of the People of Nephi. The Myth of the Ayar Brothers continues with the death of Ayar Cachi, one of the brothers who falls into a hole or cave and is buried and then later turns into a condor and appears unto them. The Legend of the Ayar Brothers states:

The Death of Ayar Cachi

"After living for some time in this place (Ollantaytambo), and forgetting about Ayar Cachi, one day, they saw him come flying towards them on huge wings of painted feathers; the brothers, fearing his sudden appearance, wanted to flee, but he took their dread from them, saying: 'Don't be worried or afraid because I have only come to tell you that now is the time when the power our Father gave us will begin to be known. That is why you should leave this place and following that good road you will come to another valley, where you should found a great city and build a sumptuous temple in which to worship the Sun. I will always pray to Wiracocha on your behalf so that you will achieve your lordship quickly and, so that you remember me forever, on a hilltop quite near here, I will remain in stone in this form in which you see me now, (as a condor).... We have seen this good sign and the world will no longer be covered with water; we have reached the summit and from here, we will choose where we should found our town!...Later, they went a little further on that mountain and, when they tried to pierce the earth with the staff of gold, the Tupayauri, it sank into the soil and stuck there so that no one could pull it out again. It was then that, looking out from this place, Manco Capac (Ayar Manco) saw a pile of rock....to mark the possession of the place,

Figure #2 Artist's rendition of the Condor mountain at Pisac, carved out of rock to remember the story of Ayar Cachi (Sam) and that he will watch over them and keep them safe.

Picture #7 Actual picture of the Pisac mountain with its carved condor and terraces.

which in the old tongue was called Cusco. This is the name of that great city, which in time became the capital of the Inca Empire." Ref 1. p.43

This legend could be the key to the mystery in the Book of Mormon surrounding Sam, the older brother of Nephi, and his progeny, and why his tribe or name is never mentioned again. It appears that he never actually reached the City of Nephi with the rest of the family. His untimely demise or accidental death would be a good reason that his family became part of Nephi's family and was amalgamated forever together with the family of

THE CITY OF NEPHI 47

Nephi. The story of Ayar Cachi (Sam) could be the explanation of this very curious mystery in the Book of Mormon.

Tree of Life

One of the great symbols of the ancient Nazca race, the 'Tree of Life', is carved on the side of a hill overlooking the Pacific Ocean at the Paracas National Reserve, which is 20 miles south of modern day Lima, Peru. It can be seen easily from one of the many boat cruises offered in the area. Some

Picture #8
The 'Tree of Life', is a famous Nazca Line, at the Paracas National Reserve.

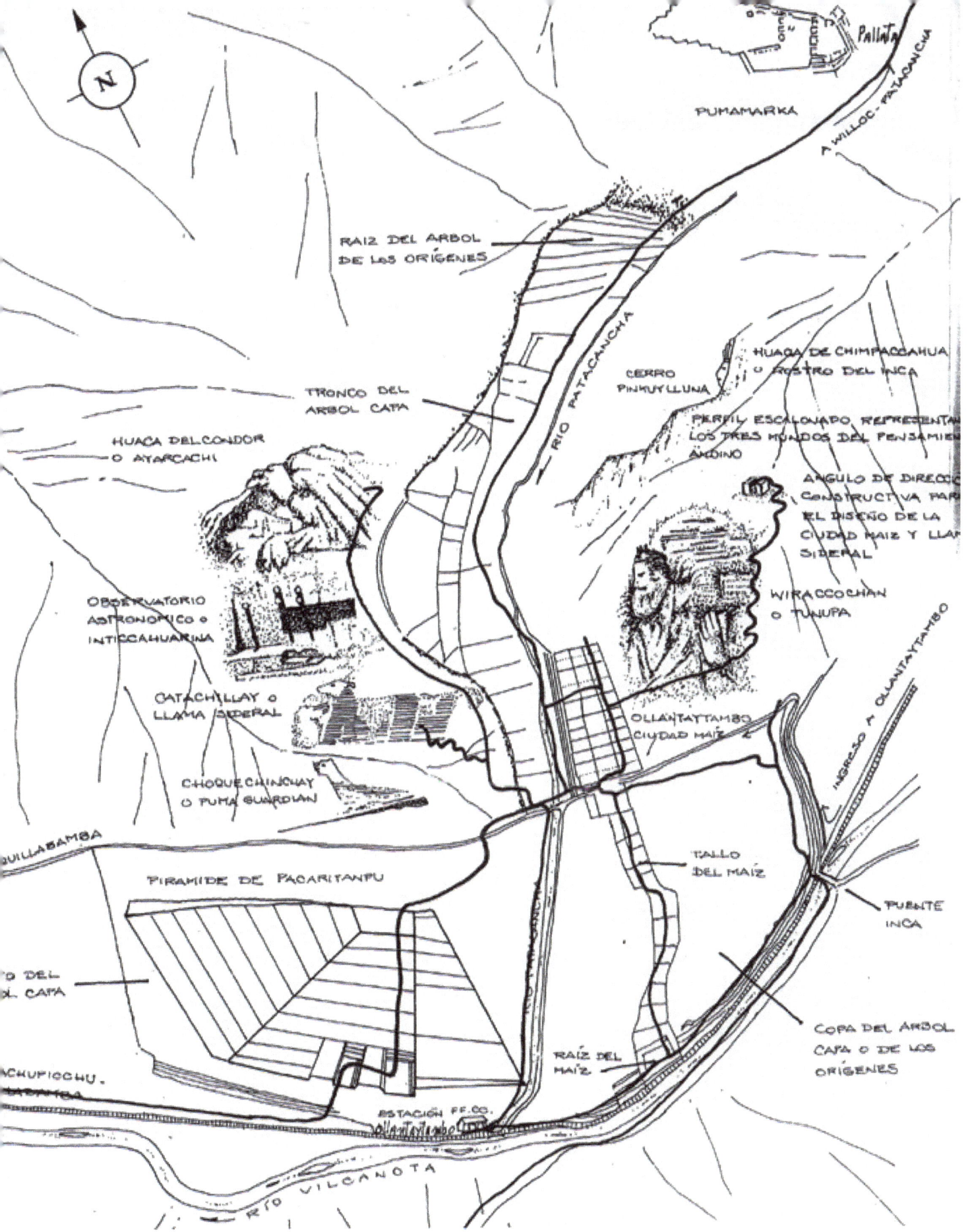

Figure #3 Diagram of the 'Tree of Life' in the Sacred Valley near Cusco encompassing the pyramid of Pacaritanpu.

call it the 'Medora' (Jewish candlestick) and others the 'Tree of Life' with the fruit to Eternal Life.

Part of the Sacred Valley also contains a very interesting legend in the form of a tree. In the top of the tree is a pyramid called Pacaritanpu. This pyramid contains windows which at certain times of the year, solstice and equinox, light up and tell the Inca farmers when it is time to plant, and harvest etc. The 'Tree of Life Legend' is extremely important with regards to the Book of Mormon and the teachings of both the prophet Lehi and his son, Nephi. The revelation in 1 Nephi 8:1-10 about the 'Tree of Life' had a profound effect on both prophets for the rest of their lives and they no doubt taught their children about it several times and rehearsed it over and over again so that they would not forget it.

Significantly, the 'Tree of Life' in the Sacred Valley just north of Cuzco, was discovered and written about nearly four hundred years ago. This area in the Sacred Valley is deemed to be the origin of life or where the Inca originated. The native Chronicler, Juan Santacruz Pachacuti (Ref 5), in 1613 drew an ideogram which shows the two custodial trees at the sides of the Pacaritanpu, (pyramid) the place which gave origin to the Incas.

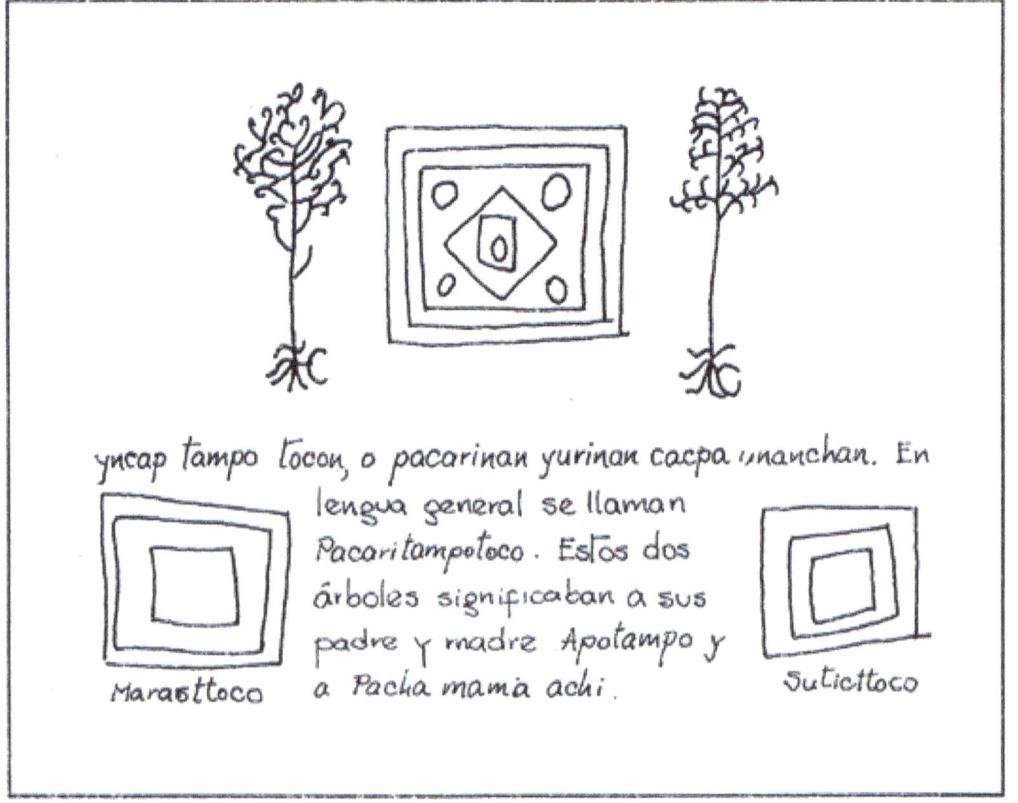

Figure #4 Ideogram of the two custodial trees, Apotampo (Father) and Pacha Mama Achi (Mother) of Pacaritanpu with the pyramid in the middle.

50 LEGENDS

Next to the figure symbolizing the Pacaritanpu, stand two trees, called the father and mother of the Inca dynasty, named Apotambo and Pachamamaachi. See the diagram on the previous page.

The Nephites had the Brass Plates which contains Genesis and Moses' story of the creation of the world, Adam and Eve, and the two famous custodial trees, the 'Tree of Knowledge of Good and Evil' and the 'Tree of Everlasting Life'. These ancient Inca and Pre-Inca peoples knew of the Creation, and Adam and Eve and chose to build this pyramid and 'Tree of Life' structure to remind their children of their origin and their sacred beginnings.

The Pisonay tree (Eritrina falcata) was planted in the main plazas in the towns throughout the valley. It is a reminder of Lehi and his dream of the 'Tree of Life'. Where the prophet sits at the base of the tree and teaches

Picture#9
A typical Village Plaza or Square in Peru seen here with huge 'Oracle Trees'.

his children as they come unto him to learn the words of eternal life. The Pisonay tree in Inca legend is an oracle or medium between God and his wise men or priests. It is a tall tree and notable for its lovely red flowers which also cause the Incas to believe it to be sacred. Ref 1.

Many of these sacred trees were believed to be oracles and were objects of continuous worship, as was mentioned by the chronicler Cieza de Leon (1553/1973:213) when he says: "…They had an oracle who answered them through the trunk of a tree, and beside it they buried gold and made sacrifices." Ref 6. There are also references to the prophet of God sitting beneath his 'great tree' and teaching his children the words of Eternal Life. Doctrinally, revelation is the means by which God speaks to his prophets and gives them guidance and instruction. To the ancient inhabitants of the Americas it was represented by the 'Tree of Life'. The tree reached upward into heaven connecting God with man and was the go-between or the intermediary. Just as in the Book of Mormon account, the prophet sat at the bottom of the tree teaching his children the gospel. A similar concept

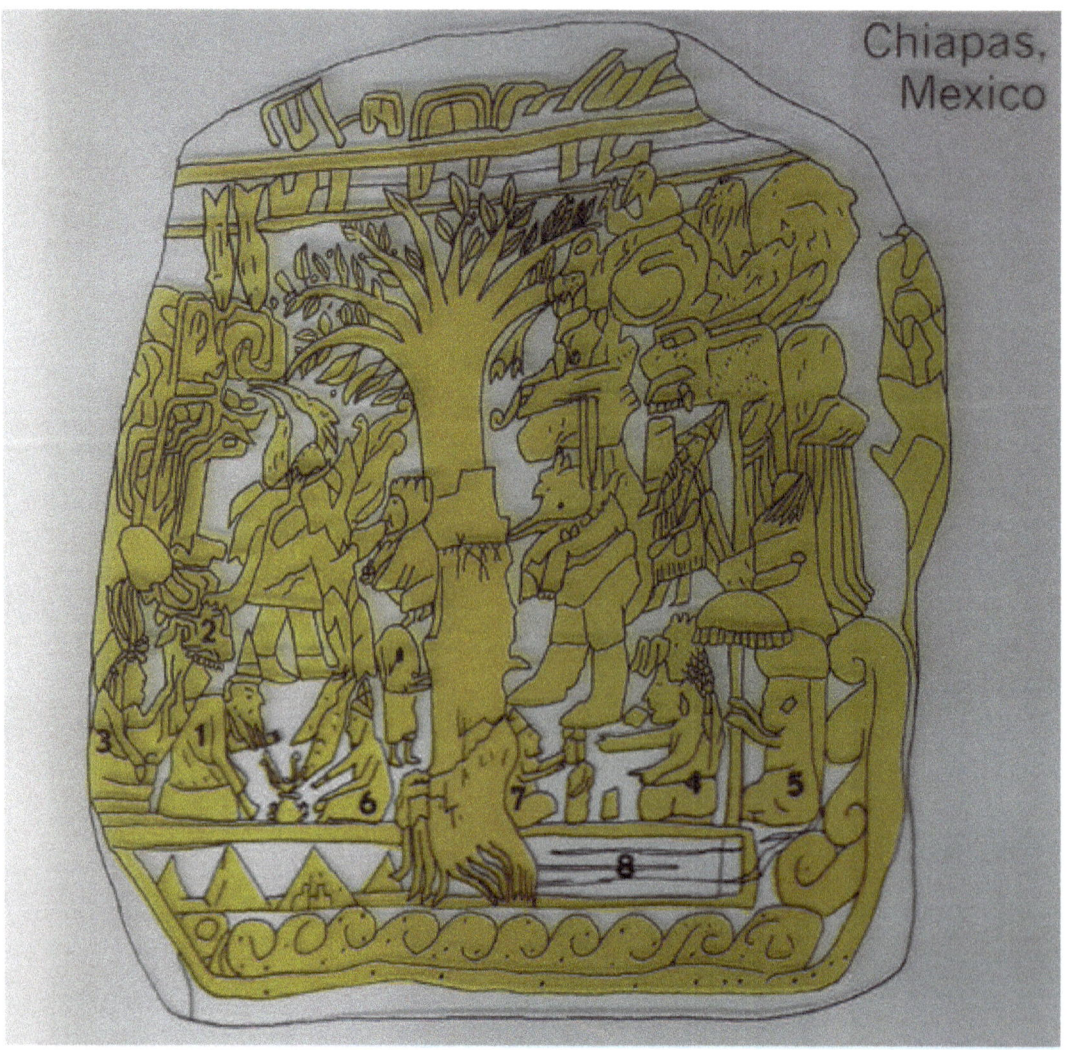

Figure #5 The 'Lehi Stone' has the small figure of Lehi (Item #7) seated at the base of the tree in the mode of teaching his children the gospel.

and diagram of this legend can be found in the stone carvings of the ancient people in Izapa, Mexico on the Stela 5 stone called the 'Lehi Stone' which depicts the prophet Lehi sitting at the base of the tree teaching his family.

The oracle legend really refers to the ancient prophets of Central and South America receiving revelation from God and then teaching these truths to the Children of Lehi.

The Pyramid of Pacaritanpu and the 'Tree of Life' in the Sacred Valley is a monumental work that encompasses an area of approximately 500 hectares and we must suppose that it took many years of continuous labor and an unflagging spirit inspired by political and religious zeal. The chronicler Juan Santacruz Pachacuti (1613), referred to the 'Tree of Life' at the Pyramid of Pacaritanpu and the first Inca Manco Capac: "….and so he (the Inca) ordered them to encase the roots with gold and silver and to hang up golden fruits because the two trees (the split tree) represented their parents which were the trunk and the root of the Incas, and they were its fruits and all this they did in order to remember its greatness." Ref 5.

Of course the fruit spoken of in the vision of the 'Tree of Life' by Nephi represented the Love of God being the fruit of the gospel. However, it easily can have many meanings and represent gospel principles of children and eternal progression, the fruits of Eternal Life. We all recognize

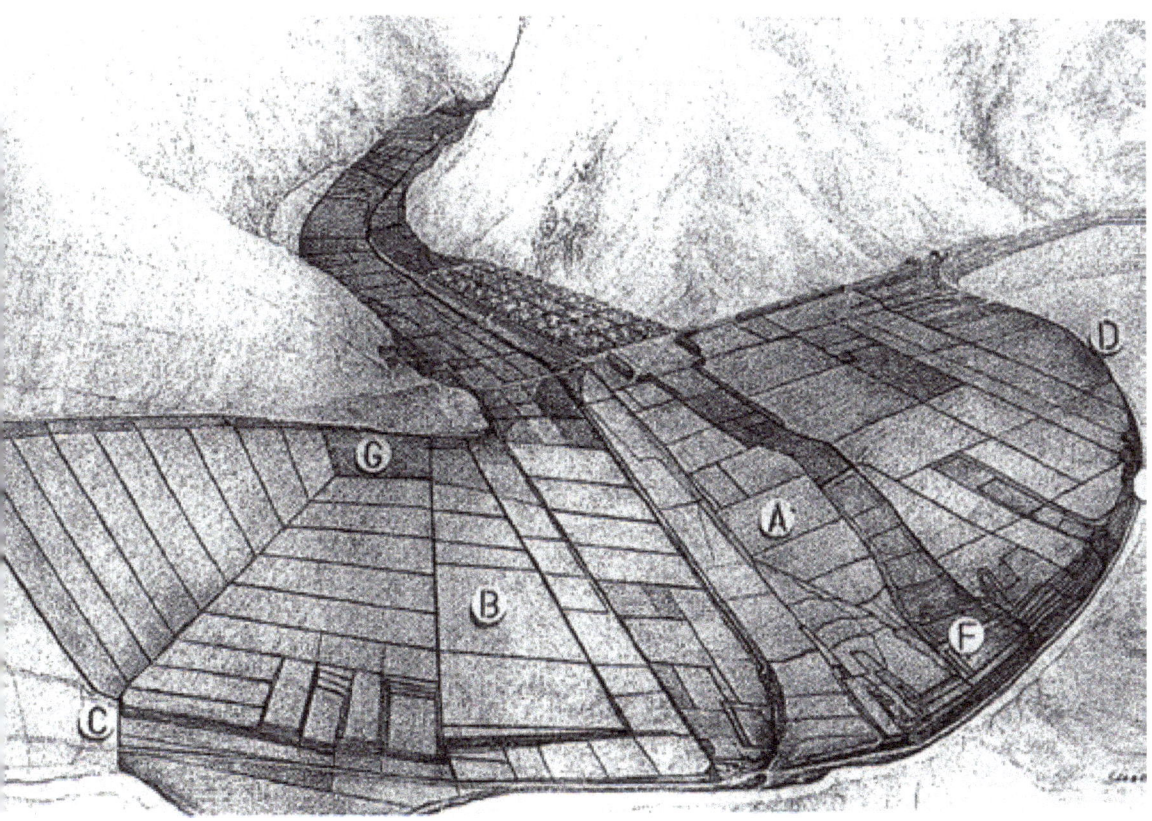

Figure #6 This is an artist's rendition of the 'Tree of Life' at Ollantaytambo. A) 'Tree of Life' with the Cob of Corn representation (Ollantaytambo). B) Face of the Pyramid of Pacaritanpu with its windows. C-E) River and irrigation canals that surround the tree. F) Base of the corn plant. G) The truncated point of the Pyramid of Pacaritanpu.

the similarities of this visionary tree to the sacred trees referred to in the Garden of Eden account. These symbols of trees then became a central concept to the theology of the Nephites, as well as the Incas.

In *The Sacred Valley of the Incas, Myths and Symbols* again a discussion of the 'Tree of Life' and the fruit is presented:

> "The grandeur and holiness created at this site reached its highest point when the fruit was planned and constructed, since this should express the most sublime example of the relationship established between man and the divine. This is why the design showed such elaborate work, making it a monument to last forever. The construction to which we are referring is none other than the Pyramid of Pacaritanpu which depicted the mythic fruit of the tree. Fruit is commonly connected to the idea of children and, by extension, the idea of continuity and regeneration. The original is contained in the seeds, and these, in turn, have the task of spreading the species throughout the world: so, in the mythic history of the Incas, the fruit of the trees was represented by the great Pacarina, the place of origin of the rulers." Ref 1.

Picture #10
Actual picture of Ollantaytambo and the Sacred Valley where the 'Tree of Life' was built into the natural landscape to remind the inhabitants of this important story forever.

54 LEGENDS

Figure #7 Incan Quipu – System of Knots to remember important facts and events.

We will present evidence and theory in the rest of this book that these ancient Nephites became the tree with its fruit being spread abroad to the northern countries of the U.S., Mexico and Central America and to the Polynesian Islands of the Pacific. They were the original tree with branches that were broken off and transplanted in other places. This small area of the Andean Highlands between Lake Titicaca and Cusco, Peru became the 'Mother of Civilization' in the New World or the 'Land of Promise' from which all other cultures and civilizations of Nephite and Lamanite affiliation had their origin. The legends of Wiracocha, Wiracochan, Manco Capac, and the 'Tree of Life' all have significant application to the Book of Mormon. These Pre-Columbian legends or myths were handed down by the 'rememberers' or Quipucamayoc (the nobles), the official Inca historians, for many generations and centuries. The Spanish Chroniclers endeavoured to write down these legends during the 16th and 17th centuries. Ancient Inca record keepers were aided by 'Quipu' which means to knot. This system of knotted strings of various colors was used to record important historical events as well as for their business accounting and monetary systems.

Obviously, there are many different accounts of the same legends and the translation from the Quechua and Aymara languages to Spanish and then later to English have caused many versions and inconsistencies. The important concepts are common to all and some truth still exists in the various legends that have been handed down to our modern days.

THE CITY OF NEPHI 55

Chapter Notes:
1. Wiracocha means 'God' or 'Supreme Being' and can also be spelled Viracocha. We add our own name of 'Our Heavenly Father' to this word usage of Wiracocha. Adding an 'n' at the end of the word to Wiracocha(n) means the 'Son of God', and we literally refer to him as Jesus Christ in this manuscript. Father and Son are alike in most aspects to the Pre-Inca peoples who knew that Wiracochan was created in the image of God. So, to differentiate between the two they add an 'n' to the end of his son's name.

{Picture Facing Ch #4) The natives of South America were well known for their expertise in boat making and traveling on the water.

CHAPTER 4

TRAVELS OF NEPHI

The prophet Nephi documented very well his travels to the 'Promised Land' and the New World. Other authors have written much material as well regarding his journey. In this chapter a short summary of his travels will be discussed to point out some obvious conclusions that will help to emphasize some important truths regarding his journeyings relevant to the City of Nephi..

Nephi As A Young Boy

According to many scholars Nephi was just a young man approximately 14-16 years of age when Lehi and his family left Jerusalem in about 600 B.C. From the scriptures we get a good description of Nephi and the type of person that the young prophet was.

> "And it came to pass that I, Nephi, being exceedingly young, nevertheless being **_large in stature_**, and also having great desires to know the mysteries of God, wherefore, I did cry unto the Lord; and behold he did visit me, and did soften my heart that I did believe all the words which had been spoken by my father…

> And it came to pass that the Lord spake unto me saying: Blessed art thou, Nephi, because of thy faith, for thou hast sought me diligently, with lowliness of heart.
>
> And inasmuch as ye shall keep my commandments, ye shall prosper, and shall be led to a land of promise; yea, even a land which I have prepared for you; yea, a land which is choice above all other lands....
>
> And inasmuch as thou shalt keep my commandments, thou shalt be made a ruler and a teacher over thy brethren." 1Nephi 2: 16, 19,20, 22

Also again when Nephi and his brethren went back to Jerusalem to get the Brass Plates he had an encounter with Laban's servant Zoram in which he said of himself:

> "And now I, Nephi, being a man **large in stature**, and also having received much strength of the Lord, therefore I did seize upon the servant of Laban, and held him, that he should not flee." 1Nephi 4:31

Nephi was a young boy but obviously large enough in stature to put on and wear the clothes and armour of the older, mature man, Laban. Nephi is most assuredly comparing his physical presence to the rest of his family and acquaintances. The large stature of Nephi could have spawned a genetic race of physically larger people that were able to dominate the usually more numerous Lamanites in battle, especially with the Lord's help. We will discuss this concept more in later chapters. We know that Nephi believed in the words of his father and did not rebel against him. It was not blind faith, but knowledge and obedience that came from divine personal revelation that helped Nephi become a leader among his brethren and in his family. Revelation was also responsible for him knowing where they were going, namely the 'Promised Land', and why.

> "And it came to pass that the angel said unto me: Look, and behold thy seed, and also the seed of thy brethren. And I looked and beheld the land of promise; and I beheld multitudes of people, yea, even as it were in number as many as the sand of the sea." 1Nephi 12:1

W. Cleon Skousen in his book, *Treasures From The Book of Mormon* points out that Nephi's father, Lehi, was probably a merchant selling and transporting goods to and from Jerusalem to Egypt and other important lands. (Volume 1 p.1019 *Portrait of Lehi*) Ref 12. Lehi was extremely wealthy in silver and gold and precious things. The question as to why a prophet of God would have so many of these kinds of possessions and wealth are probably because they were trade goods or wealth necessary for his business. He was possibly even a merchant of precious metals. He most likely was affiliated with gold and silversmiths and the industry of metallurgy. As a young boy, Nephi, no doubt had opportunity to travel on these business trips to Egypt and other places. This is important to consider in light of the fact that Nephi was taught Egyptian as well as his native Hebrew, and understood how to write in a modified form of ancient Egyptian symbols that could be used for record keeping. The names of Nephi and Sam are Egyptian and so Egypt had a great impact on Nephi as a young boy. Also, as part of his education as a youth, he might have received training in metallurgy for making tools, metal plates, swords, etc., as part of the family merchant business. On trips to Egypt he could have become familiar with the art of stone cutting, building, and the working of huge cyclopean or monolithic blocks of stone. He was no doubt familiar with the Temple of Solomon in Jerusalem and the great pyramids of Egypt. Nephi's education and experiences as a youth would be the foundation of his knowledge that would help him in future years as the leader of his followers and the builder of a nation.

The use of such huge stones of 100-300 tons for ancient construction occurs only in a few places in the world today. In Jerusalem at the base or foundation of the temple mount such stones can be seen via the modern tunnel of the Western Wall. The ancient pyramids of Egypt have polygonal foundation stones that weigh in excess of 100 tons, fit together perfectly without mortar. Several places in the Cusco area of Peru such building stones have also been incorporated in the Pre-Inca construction. Sacsahuaman, Ollantaytambo, Cusco, and Machu Pichu are just of few of the ruins in the Andean area that such cyclopean architecture can be seen today. That alone gives much evidence that the cultures are at least related somehow.

The Marriage of Nephi

The second task that the sons of Lehi were asked to do after retrieving the Plates of Brass from Jerusalem, was to go back after the family of

Ishmael. We know that while in the Valley of Lemuel, a few days journey into the wilderness from Jerusalem, he married a daughter of Ishmael. Nephi does not write a lot about his wife or his personal life. We only know that she intervened on his behalf on more than one occasion to soften the hearts of his wicked brethren.

> 19. "And it came to pass that they were angry with me again, and sought to lay hands upon me; but behold, one of the daughters of Ishmael, yea, and also her mother, and one of the sons of Ishmael, did plead with my brethren, insomuch that they did soften their hearts; and they did cease striving to take away my life." 1Nephi 7:19

Later in Chapter 16 of 1Nephi, Nephi records these words about his marriage:

> 7. And it came to pass that I, Nephi, took one of the daughters of Ishmael to wife; and also, my brethren took of the daughters of Ishmael to wife; and also Zoram took the eldest daughter of Ishmael to wife." 1Nephi 16:7

Nephi's wife was stalwart and strong in her faith and ever devoted to Nephi and stood by him through all his problems with his older brothers. Nephi writes:

> 19. "…..and also my wife with her tears and prayers, and also my children, did not soften the hearts of my brethren that they would loose me." 1Nephi 18:19

Jerusalem to the Land Bountiful

They journeyed Southward along the Red Sea into the desert of the Arabian Peninsula being led by the Liahona and their faith. Nephi was, however, very concerned about his family and his wife and her personal welfare and suffering like any good husband would be. Nephi writes the following:

> "And it came to pass that we did return without food to our families, and being much fatigued, because of their journeying, they did suffer much for the want of food." 1Nephi 16:19

Later, after the death of Ishmael in the wilderness, Lehi's party changes direction in their travels. In Chapter 17 Nephi recounts:

> "And it came to pass that we did again take our journey in the wilderness; and we did travel nearly eastward from that time forth. And we did travel and wade through much affliction in the wilderness; and our women did bear children in the wilderness." 1Nephi 17:1

Finally, they reached the 'Land Bountiful' after much trial and tribulation. See the next map of their proposed travels upon the Arabian Peninsula. Nephi says simply:

> "And we did sojourn for the space of many years, yea, even **eight years** in the wilderness." 1Nephi 17:4

It took Nephi and his family **eight long years** to travel **2500 miles** around the Arabian Peninsula. Some days they probably made good progress, maybe 10-20 miles per day, but they obviously had to stop and rest a lot as well because of birthing mothers, little children, burying their dead, and hunting, etc. See map in Figure #8 for the possible route that Lehi's party took to reach the 'Land Bountiful'.

Building a Ship

In the 'Land Bountiful' the leadership situation changes considerably because the Lord commands Nephi to build a ship. It's interesting that the Lord asked Nephi to build the ship at this point and not his father, Lehi. The Prophet Lehi would have been older by then and the Lord undoubtedly needed Nephi's youthful strength and energy for the project.

> "And it came to pass that after I, Nephi, had been in the land of Bountiful for the space of **many days**, the voice of the Lord came unto me, saying: Arise, and get thee into the mountain. And it came to pass that I arose and went up into the mountain, and cried unto the Lord." 1Nephi 17:7

The key words that Nephi uses in his account here are 'for the space of **many days**.' We will see later in the chapter that Nephi uses these same words to describe the length of time his family traveled into the wilderness to find and establish the City of Nephi.

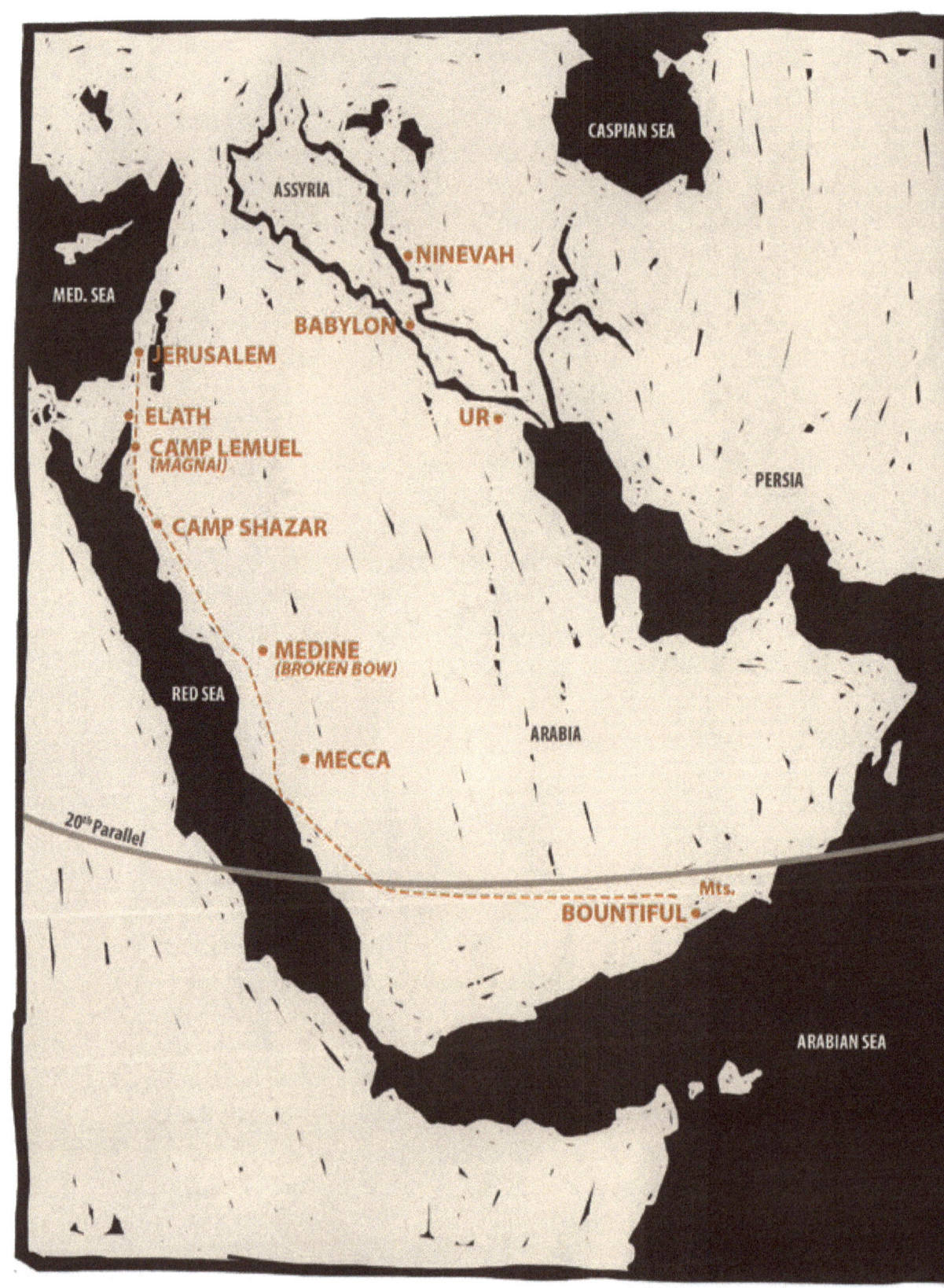

Figure #8 Map of the Arabian Peninsula and the travels of the Lehi colony for eight years in the wilderness to the 'Land Bountiful'.

TRAVELS OF NEPHI

Picture #11
Nephi or Manco Capac at the Cusco fortress in the Promised Land.

Ocean Voyage to the Promised Land

Again Nephi uses the term '**many days**' twice more to describe the length of time they sailed on their journey.

"…we did put forth into the sea and were driven forth before the wind towards the Promised Land. And after we had

THE CITY OF NEPHI

been driven forth before the wind for the space of **many days**, behold…." 1Nephi 18:8-9

This account was presumably written many years later after Nephi was living happily in his new land, possibly even thirty years later. So, it is compelling that he is so specific as to his references of time. On the oceanic journey his brothers and their wives make themselves merry and offend God. Nephi is taken captive, the compass ceases to work, and a great storm drives them back for **three days**. The boat is then on the fourth day nearly swallowed up in the depths of the sea. 1Nephi 18:13-15 Because of the fear of death, they loose Nephi of his bonds and he is able to direct the ship with the aid of the Liahona again to the Promised Land.

"And it came to pass that after we had sailed for the space of **many days** we did arrive at the promised land…" 1Nephi 18:23

He used the term '**many days**' twice on the voyage, once before the storm and once after the storm. Some scholars have suggested that the ocean voyage took the family of Lehi approximately a year. It also took the Brother of Jared and his group a similar amount of time though their routes were most likely very different.

Many Days

The term '*many days*' is used by Nephi several times in his writings. Where there are short periods of days that can be counted, he is very specific to count the days for us. If it is a long period of time of more than a year in length, Nephi is very specific in the number of years. Trying to put the time period '*many days*' into a more specific amount of time is difficult, because each time he used this term the length of time he referred to was probably a little different. However, it can be suggested that '*many days*' was probably at least 170-200 days. We know that when Lehi's family got to the 'Land Bountiful' they planted their seeds and then would have harvested their crops before they boarded their new ship, so that they would have had fresh provisions for their ocean voyage. It would have taken at least 120 days for those crops to mature. At first Nephi would have been preoccupied with planting and nurturing his crop, before he could take time to build the boat. 170 days before the storm incident on the ocean crossing and approximately 170 days after the storm would satisfy somewhat the time interval of '*many days*' if the crossing took almost a year.

The Promised Land

When Lehi's family got to the Promised Land, Lehi immediately gave thanks to the Lord. They established themselves in the 'Promised Land' and again planted their seeds and cultivated their crops for a season. The landing area north of Santiago, Chile at Coquimbo is arid and dry. But the hill country and valleys leading up into the Andean ranges are fertile with many rivers to irrigate the crops. Some of the best fruit orchards and vegetable gardens in South America can be found in this region. Lehi grew old and blessed his children and grandchildren before he died. After the death of the family patriarch as so often happens, the unity and cohesiveness of the family disappeared; and Nephi and his followers were forced to flee into the wilderness for their safety.

Journey to the City of Nephi

Nephi, or Manco Capac, then began his epic journey into the wilderness that has been chronicled by the 'rememberers' in the legends. Probably between 590 to 585 B.C. Nephi says that they took their belongings and journeyed for '*many days*' into the wilderness. In the previous discussion, it was suggested a time period of about 170-200 days journey was equivalent to the term '*many days*'. Averaging some 10-20 miles per day maximum with provisions and presumably small children would be a difficult journey. This would be even more difficult if the terrain was uphill, mountainous, and with no roads or maps; especially carrying all your possessions and provisions with you. Tending herds and hunting for food and water along the way would have slowed their progress as well. If they travelled approximately 24-29 weeks (170-200 days) as our '*many days*' definition allows, then they probably could have traveled between 600 to 1450 miles if they traveled an average of five days a week and had two rest days a week.

The direction of travel according to our map was northward and into the mountainous regions of the Andes. Leaving or escaping Laman and Lemuel (the Lamanites), and their original settlements in the Land Southward, on the Pacific coast of Chile had to be done quickly. Nephi and his little band most likely stayed along the coast to begin with as they went north. This would have given them their best advantage to quickly distance themselves from the Lamanites who would surely be following after them. Eventually, they would turn east and climb up into the Andes and the Lake Titicaca region. Today this proposed route for Nephi from Coquimbo, Chile to Cusco, Peru (our proposed location of the City of

Nephi) is just over a thousand mile. This distance could definitely be done within the '***many days***' scenario of our theory. However, to imagine that the state of New York could be accessed from the original landing (some 7000 miles distance) within Nephi's description of the events is impossible. Remember, that the Nephite party sent out by King Limhi from the City of Nephi in search of Zarahemla, were lost for '***many days***' searching the Land Northward. They saw the areas of the Jaredite destruction and found the record of Ether. This is the same area presumably where the true Hill Cumorah and the final Nephite battle took place. If Nephi would have traveled further north into the wilderness, then, he would have told us how many years it took instead of using the '***many days***' term. He was well familiar already with their eight year, 2500 mile trek in the wilderness across the deserts of the Arabian Peninsula. See Figure #9 for the map of the probable route of Nephi and his followers.

Nephi relates the following about their journey in the wilderness:

> 7. And we did take our tents and whatsoever things were possible for us, and did journey in the wilderness for the space of ***many days***. And after we had journeyed for the space of ***many days*** we did pitch our tents.
>
> 8. And my people would that we should call the name of the place Nephi; wherefore, we did call it Nephi. 2Nephi 5:7-8

Garcilaso de la Vega, a Spanish chronicler, (Ref 3.) wrote that Manco Capac and his sister-wife, between them, taught the people and established laws and a government. They taught their people methods of agriculture and introduced arts and a textile industry to clothe themselves. 3.Garcilaso de la Vega, The Incas, 1539-1616 translated by Maria Jolas. The Book of Mormon says of the followers of the prophet Nephi:

> 11. "And the Lord was with us; and we did prosper exceedingly; for we did sow seed, and we did reap again in abundance. And we began to raise flocks, and herds, and animals of every kind.
>
> 13. And it came to pass that we began to prosper exceedingly, and to multiply in the land.
>
> 15. I did teach my people to build buildings, and to work in all manner of wood, and of iron, and of copper, and of brass, and

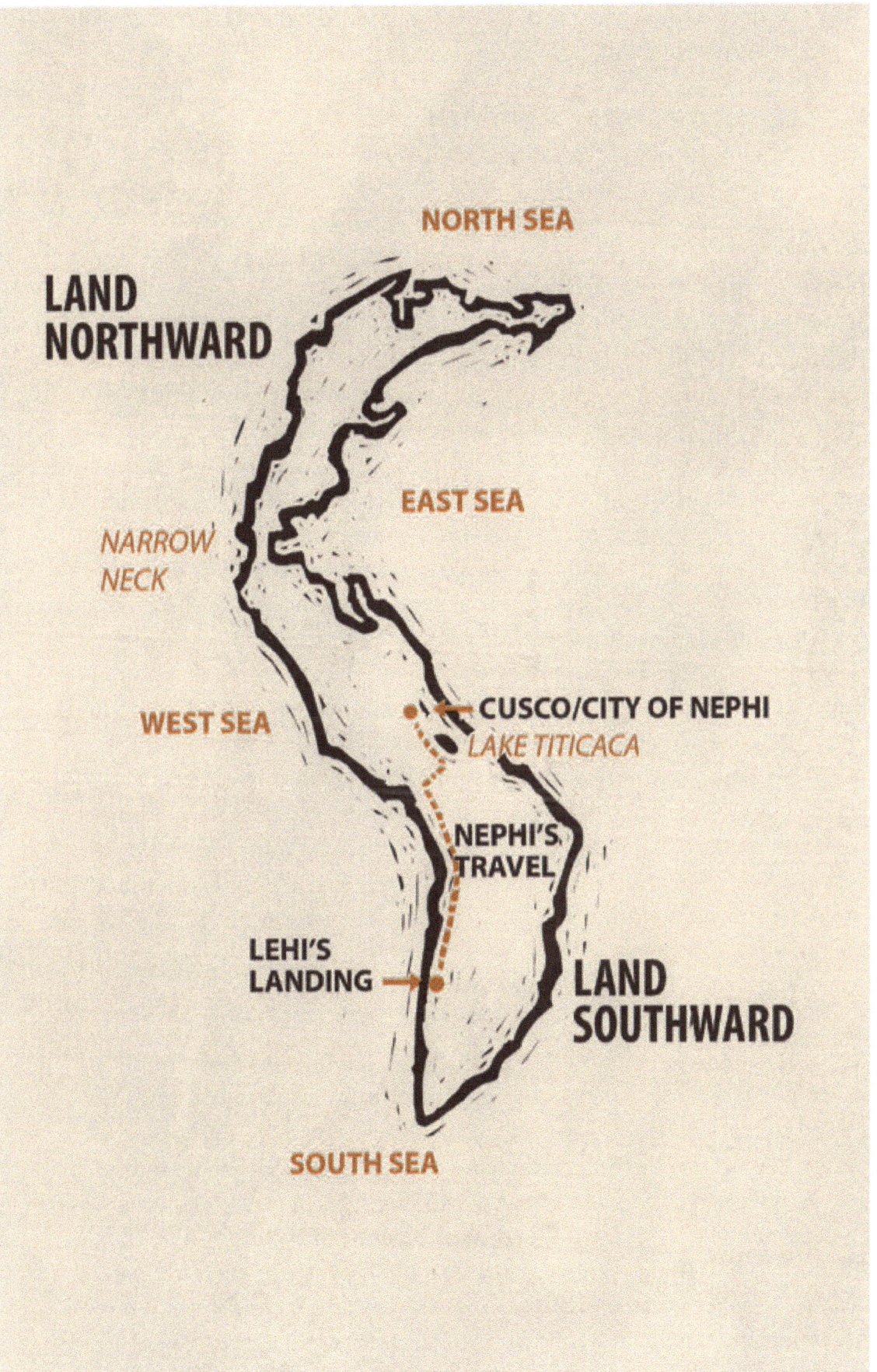

Figure #9 Map showing Nephi's travel from their first landing in the 'Promised Land' to the eventual City of Nephi (Cusco, Peru), a little over a thousand mile journey.

THE CITY OF NEPHI

of steel, and of gold, and of silver, and of precious ores, which were in great abundance.

17. And it came to pass that I, Nephi, did cause my people to be industrious, and to labor with their hands." 2Nephi 5:11, 13, 15 & 17.

Nephi in the City of Nephi

Nephi writes very little more about the land or his travels during the last years of his life. We know that Nephi died 55 years after they left Jerusalem (600 B.C.) in about 545 B.C. So, being in the wilderness for eight years, and then in Bountiful for months, crossing the ocean for a year, and traveling to the City of Nephi all account for probably at least ten years. Most likely this would leave the prophet Nephi 45 years to build his city and temple in the Land of Nephi. Of course one can imagine that such a great prophet would build most likely a great civilization. We also know that since Nephi was a righteous prophet and king, he would not have subjected his people to burdensome taxes or labor to complete facilities that were not needed or important to their survival. And Nephi could only build according to the resources at his disposal. He had limited manpower when they first arrived in the City of Nephi. Labor to build buildings, irrigation canals, fortresses, and etc. would have been modest to say the least. However, we can rightly suggest that many projects and buildings were at least started and cities and highways planned during the days of Nephi. The actual grandeur of the city in the Land of Nephi would have progressed throughout the Nephite 450 year occupation of the Land of Nephi.

Population Growth

The population growth to feed the labor pool would determine actually how much would be accomplished during Nephi's life time. We can estimate that Nephi, Sam, and Zoram each had an average of five children upon their arrival in the Land of Nephi. Because Jacob and Joseph and Nephi's two younger sisters were still teenagers or young children when they got to the City of Nephi then we will count them just as individuals. This estimate would only give us a group of 25 people at their time of arrival. Lehi and Sarah could have had as many as ten children. We don't know for sure. So, if all of these pioneer families were large like Lehi's family and we said an average of eight children to be conservative, then the first generation would be three families of eight children or 24 children plus four more of Nephi's brothers and sisters making 28 children and 34 total people with the adults. In the second generation if all of these children paired up to make 14 couples, and they had eight children each, that would make 112 children plus the 34 from the first generation or probably around 146 people. These 112 children would make 56 couples with an average of five children would make 280 children in the third generation plus the married couples and the older generations would make the population well over 300 people at the time of the death of Nephi. Obviously, the fourth and fifth generation, the population numbers would really take off. But during the lifetime of Nephi the population would be fairly modest especially factoring in problems with disease, accidents, and wars, and thus the opportunity for building a grand city and civilization would actually be a product of future generations.

Summary of Nephi's Life and Travels

Contemplating the mark and the significance of the life of the great prophet leaders in the history of this world is a worthwhile exercise. Nephi had less resources than many other prophet leaders. These leaders had more people to accomplish more significant projects and build cities from the rudiments of the wilderness with only the elements and their bare hands. to work with than did Nephi. Joseph Smith and Brigham Young had more people and more technology to work with than did Nephi. We still know that Nephi was able to accomplish much with the help of the Lord and his small band. Ten years he spent wandering in the wilderness before he found his 'Promised Land', the Center of his Universe, and what would become to his people the 'Navel of his World'. Out of the wilderness, he was able to forge a new life, a new city, and a magnificent temple to God. His brother Jacob said of him:

> 10. "The people having **loved** Nephi exceedingly, he having been a great protector for them, having wielded the sword of Laban in their defence, and having labored in all his days for their welfare—" Jacob 1:10

What actually could be said more of the prophet king, Nephi, than that his people loved him. It is the best tribute that can be given, and shows truly the qualities that this man of God possessed.

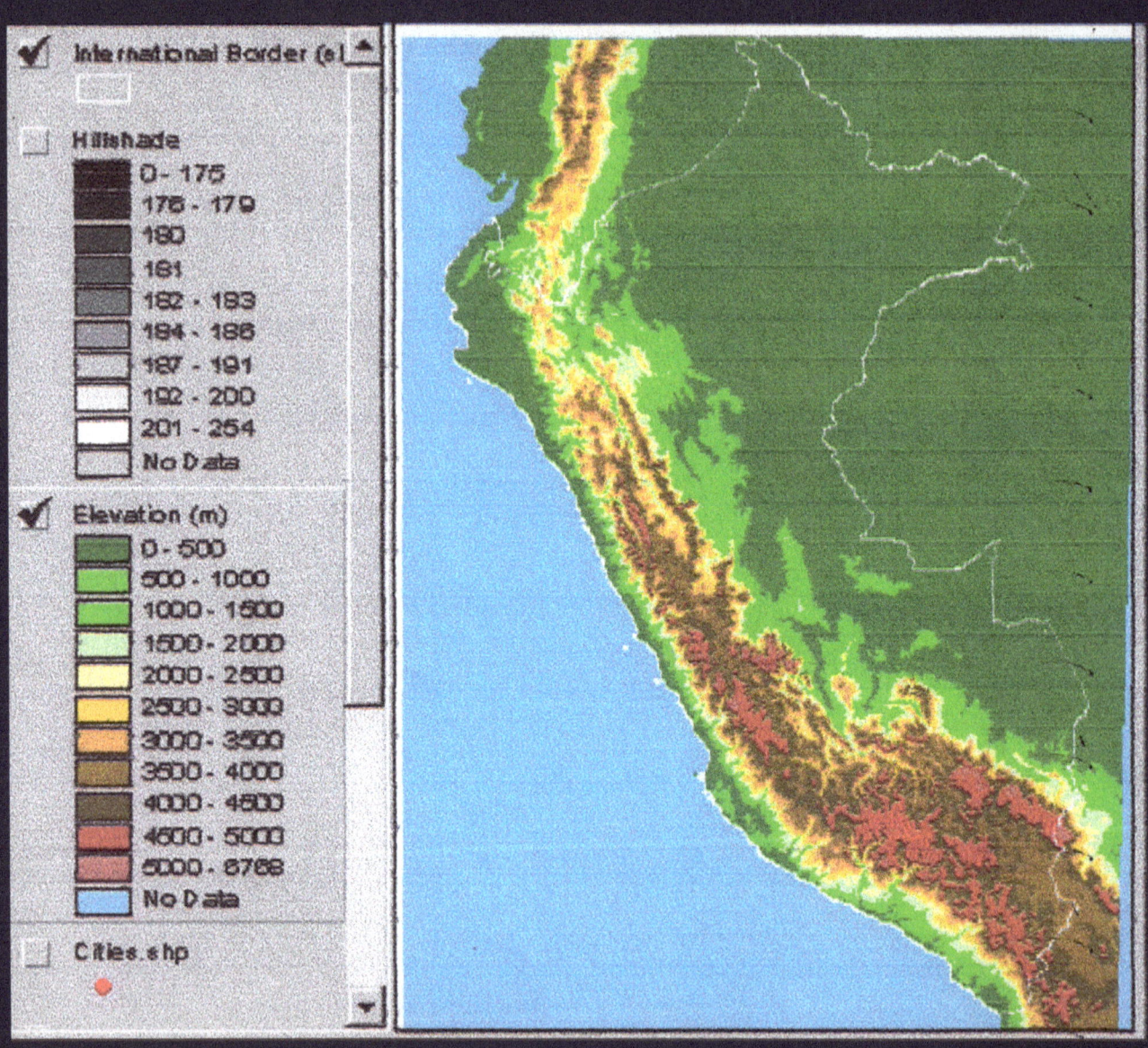

{Facing Picture Ch #5) In this topographical map with elevations, the long narrow island of the Promised Land is evident with the narrow neck at the Gulf of Guayaquil.

CHAPTER 5

BOOK OF MORMON GEOGRAPHY

The Book of Mormon geography is a compelling topic; and a very controversial one with most Book of Mormon students. We have to start on some common ground to be able to discuss some future subjects. There are so many theories and books written about this subject, do we really need another one until there is more light given on the geography? Most of us say yes, and we can't get enough of it. We feel we will finally get more information from the Lord if we continue to read, study, and petition Him about it. So, we'll dive right in and start with **Lehi's Landing** and present what we will call in this book the **Changed Land Theory**. Then we can discuss what the land was like **Before the Coming of Christ** and then how it now looks **After the Coming of Jesus Christ** to the Americas.

LEHI'S LANDING

Most scholars admit and believe that there is not much evidence and very little said by Joseph Smith and other early Church leaders about the actual voyage and landing of Lehi and his family in the Americas. However, we present here several of the many references to the actual location of the landing of Lehi's party. All these references are specific about South America. The first reference to discuss comes from the *Compendium* by James A. Little and Franklin D. Richards (Salt Lake City: Deseret News 1912 edition, but copyright 1882 p. 289 Ref 7.) it states:

> "Lehi's Travels – Revelation to Joseph the Seer. The course that Lehi and his company traveled from Jerusalem to the place of their destination: They traveled nearly a south southeast direction until they came to the nineteenth degree of north latitude; then nearly east to the Sea of Arabia, then sailed in a southeast direction, and Landed on the continent of South America, in Chile, Thirty degrees south latitude." Ref 7.

This is the exact quote from our source document and #1 truth from Chapter one on Truths or the revelation given to Joseph Smith presumably in the Kirtland Temple and written down by Frederick G. Williams in the School of the Prophets. This first quote seems to justify or substantiate the original document in the Church Archives for sure.

Dr. John Bernhisel

The second reference also has the exact same wordage, but from a completely different source, this time from Dr. John Bernhisel, who was a close friend of Joseph Smith and Bishop of the LDS ward in New York City. Dr. Bernhisel went to visit Emma Smith after the death of Joseph Smith and made a copy of Joseph's revision of the Bible by copying notes into his own KJV Bible. The last page of the manuscript contains the following exact same quote:

> **"The course that Lehi traveled from the city of Jerusalem to the place where he and his family took ship, they traveled nearly a south southeast direction until they came to the nineteenth degree of North latitude, then nearly east to the sea of Arabia then sailed in a south east direction and landed on the continent of South America in Chili thirty degrees south of lattitude." Ref 31**

This quote was written down by Bernhisel from the Revised Bible Manuscript that was in the possession of Emma Smith directly from the Bible revelations document known as the 'Joseph Smith Translation' (JST) made by Joseph Smith. Bernhisel spent much of the spring of 1845 working on this project. The LDS Church has Bernhisel's Bible in its archives, but it contains less than half of the corrections and is not suitable for publication. For many years the "Bernhisel Bible" was the only JST source for the LDS Church members living in the Salt Lake Valley.

Orson Pratt

The third reference is made by Orson Pratt who was the Church Historian and wrote an article for an encyclopedia in 1874 where he expressed the same truth more fully, stating that the landing took place, "as believed, not far from the 30th degree south latitude." (See <u>Millennial Star</u>, Vol, 38, pp.691-692). The 30th parallel on the western side of the continent would be near the present day location of Coquimbo, Chile. The forth reference to the landing was made also by Orson Pratt, who was a close friend to the Prophet and an apostle in 1840. He says that Lehi "landed upon the western coast of South America". (Orson Pratt,-- *Remarkable Visions*) Ref 9.

In the book, *Masterful Discourses and Writings of Orson Pratt* by N.B. Lundwall, Elder Pratt makes more than five references to the location of the Lehi landing in South America in his discourses in chapter 6. At the funeral services of this great man, President Wilford Woodruff said in 1881, "....Brother Pratt had lived longer in the Church, traveled more miles, and preached more sermons than any man in it. He had baptised thousands, and fulfilled the revelation given to him through the Prophet Joseph Smith, November 4, 1830. His garments were clean from the blood of this generation. He had studied and written more upon the Gospel and upon science than any other man in the Church." Ref. 27

Also, there have been other non specific references in the <u>Times and Seasons</u> (Sept 15, 1842, Vol. 3:921-922) written while Joseph Smith was alive and while he was the Editor stating that "….. Lehi went down by the Red Sea to the great Southern Ocean, and crossed over to this land, and landed a little south of the Isthmus of Darien, and improved the country…." These landing references that we know about clearly are all in South America and have **<u>Lehi and his family disembarking in South America and in Chile, at the 30th parallel</u>**, which is a significant phenomenon. Other references to substanciate this important truth discovery come from these important Church leaders as follows:

George Q. Cannon

George Q. Cannon was an apostle and member of the First Presidency for four prophets and in his book, *The Life of Nephi, the Son of Lehi.* he wrote the following:

"The Prophet Joseph, in speaking of their place of landing, said, "It was on the coast of the country now known as Chili – a country which possesses a genial, temperate climate." They traveled nearly a south, southeast direction until they came to the nineteenth degree of north latitude; then, nearly east to the sea of Arabia, then sailed in a southeast direction, and landed on the continent of South America, in Chili, thirty degrees south latitude. They immediately turned their attention to agriculture. They prepared the ground and put in all the seeds which they had brought with them from the land of Jerusalem. They found the soil admirable adapted for agriculture. Their seeds grew finely and yielded good crops, and they were blessed with abundance." Ref. 29

Frederick G. Williams

Frederick G. Williams, who presumably wrote down our Source Document #1 while taking notes in the School of the Prophets in Kirtland as they proceeded from the mouth of the prophet was Joseph Smith's scribe and close friend. He is said to also have had a vision of the Lehi landing place, in the Kirtland Temple. His son, Frederick Salem Williams had this to say about his father and what happened:

"Frederick Granger Williams grand- and great- grandchildren have spent well over an accumulated 100 years in missionary work among the descendants of Father Lehi in Latin America. Perhaps it was prophetic that the angel showed our progenitor, Dr. Frederick Granger Williams, the vision in which he saw Lehi's landing place in South America. This vision was received in the Kirtland Temple which is constructed on land that he donated to the Church for that purpose. – Frederick Salem Williams, son." Ref.30

Parley P. Pratt

It is an interesting fact that Elder Parley P. Pratt, brother and fellow apostle to Orson Pratt received a call from President Brigham Young and the First Presidency to be President of the Pacific Mission in February of 1851. In March President Pratt proceeded to California with his company to organize and strengthen the branches of the Church there. He sent missionaries to the Sandwich Islands and other places. According to the

Autobiography of Parley P. Pratt, Ref. 28, President Pratt set sail with his wife and little group to perform the first mission of the Church to South America. They left for Valparaiso, Chile on September 5th 1851 from San Francisco on the ship 'Henry Kelsey'. They studied the Spanish language everyday on the voyage in earnest. They arrived in Valparaiso, Chile on November 8th after a very arduous two month journey with terrible food and accommodations. They had a very poor command of the language and met with very little missionary success. The whole of South America was caught up in revolutions and civil wars which did not provide a good environment for teaching the gospel. President Pratt and his companions stayed in the area until their money ran out. They boarded a ship bound for San Francisco March 2nd 1852 to return to Salt Lake City. This learning experience taught the leaders that to preach the gospel to these foreign countries the Church would need to be better prepared with the language, the Book of Mormon translated into Spanish, and an organized mission with the financial resources to accomplish the mission of the Church. Those are the facts of the first missionary attempt to South America. However, Parley P. Pratt, had opportunity to go anywhere in Mexico, Central America, or other South American countries like Peru. But, he chose to go to Northern Chile. The question really is why did he travel specifically to the 30th parallel of Chile? It was obviously a fact finding mission approved by the First Presidency and Brigham Young. All of these early Church leaders knew that it was the land of Lehi's first inheritance, the 'Promised Land'.

Dr. James E. Talmage

The last reference that we will discuss comes from the only book owned and published, on a constant basis today, by the LDS Church, where a reference is made mention of the Lehi Landing. It is in the book, *Jesus the Christ* written by Dr. James E. Talmage, who was an apostle and revered scholar, where he quotes the following:

> "….The company journeyed somewhat east of south, keeping near the borders of the Red Sea; then changing their course to the eastward, crossed the peninsula of Arabia; and there, on the shores of the Arabian Sea, built and provisioned a vessel in which they committed themselves to divine care upon the waters. Their voyage carried them eastward across the Indian Ocean, then over the south Pacific Ocean to the western coast of **South America**, whereon they landed (590 B.C.)…The people established themselves on what to them was the land of promise;

many children were born, and in the course of a few generations a numerous posterity held possession of the land….They spread northward, occupying the northern part of **South America**; then, crossing the Isthmus, they extended their domain over the southern, central and eastern portions of what is now the United States of America." Ref. 25 Jesus The Christ p. 55-56 Talmage, Chapter Note #3.

Focusing in on the continent of South America helps to define the Book of Mormon geography. Knowing where the family of Lehi landed in the Americas is crucial to the geography of the Book of Mormon, and knowing that they landed in Chile will help establish a foundation for future points of discussion. So, the LDS Church actually publishes today the fact that the landing was on the western coast of **South America**. Every missionary that goes out on a mission today uses the approved set of Missionary Reference Library which includes the book, *Jesus The Christ*, by Talmage.

OCEAN CURRENTS

Leon C. Dalton in "Routes to the Promised Land" which appeared in the Liahona, The Elders Journal, August 8, 1944 Ref 10, he writes:

> "An examination of the pilot charts of the world reveals that if the Nephites embarked in the late summer, after the harvest, they would have two or three months of northerly winds (winds out of the north) or about 100 days, and if they floated at the normal rate of from 3 to 5 miles per hour, they would reach a south latitude of about 40 degrees in that length of time, or slightly south of the line connecting Cape Town, South Africa and Melbourne, Australia. Here they would encounter the ….'Prevailing Westerlies', (winds blowing west to east) as they would here enter the ocean currents that travel eastward around the globe the year around. These currents continue their eastward course until they encounter 56 degrees south latitude, where they split. Those south of 56 degrees continue on around the earth, while those striking the Chilean coast are deflected northward along the shoreline, turning seaward again at about 35 degrees south latitude during the warm months, but continuing northward to about 20 degrees during the winter…." Ref 10.

This analysis of the ocean currents would easily have put Lehi's party at the 30 degrees south latitude in Chile where these early Church references placed the original landing.

CHANGED LAND THEORY

South American Continent before the Land was Changed

One of the most important facts to consider from the Book of Mormon is that after the death and resurrection of Christ the whole face of the land changed.

> "11. And there was a great and terrible destruction in the land southward.
>
> 12 But behold, there was a more great and terrible destruction in the land northward; for behold, the **whole face of the land was changed**, because of the tempest and the whirlwinds, and the thunderings and the lightnings, and the exceedingly great quaking of the whole earth;" 3Nephi 8:11-12

What does this mean? How could the whole face of the land change, and what would it have looked like before the change? What was it like when Lehi first set foot upon the land known as South America? Venice Priddis, in her book, *The Book and the Map* Ref 11, expounds on this theory. So, it is not peculiar or original to this work by any means. In her

Figure #10 A world map of the ocean currents shows (a green line with arrows) the departure of Lehi's ship from the Land Bountiful (Oman on the Arabian Peninsula) to the 30th Parallel on the western coast of Chile and the Promised Land.

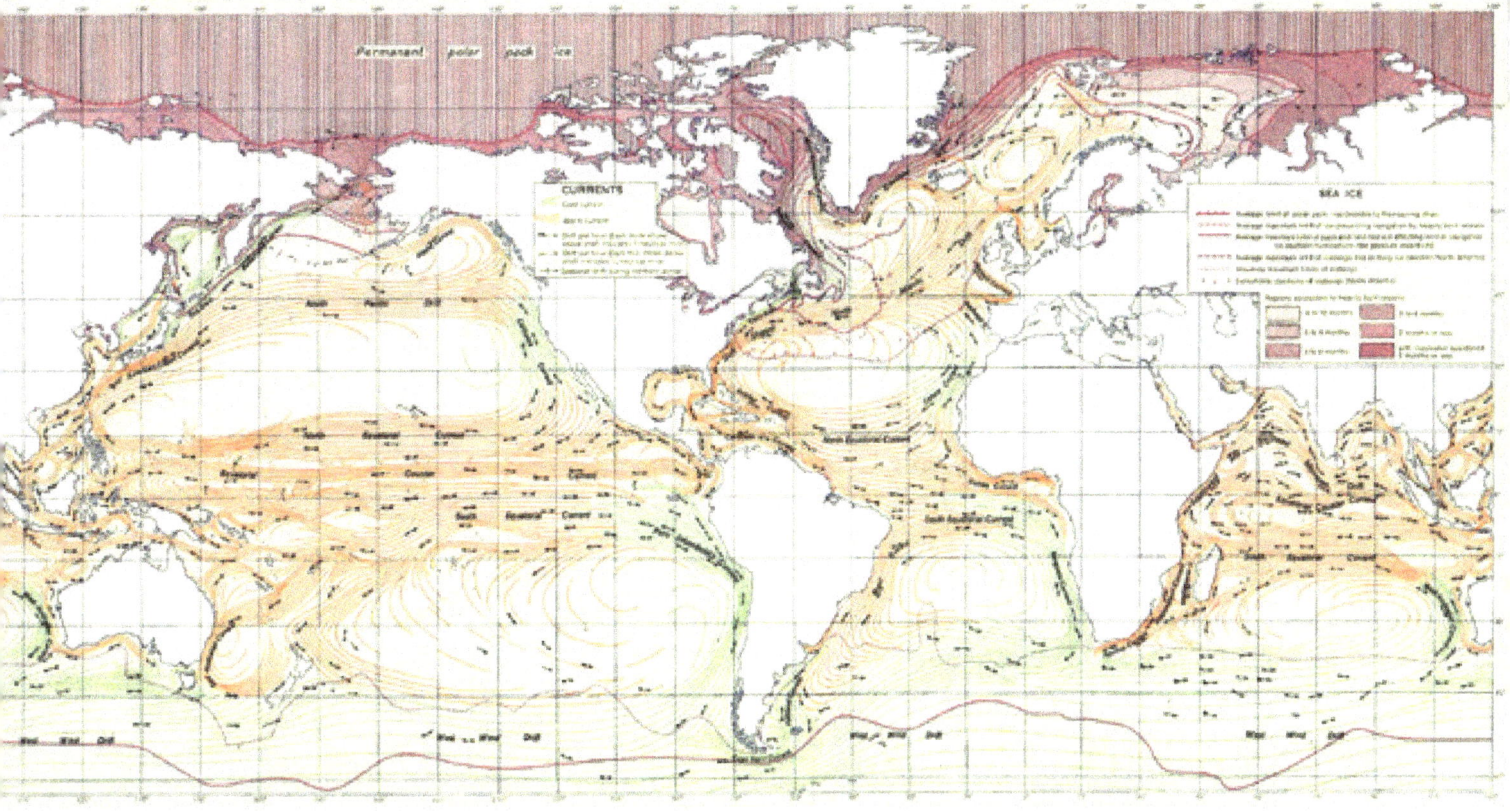

book, Priddis, states that Charles Darwin, in his historic, *Voyage of the Beagle* mapped South America and made some interesting discoveries. He found sharks teeth and petrified coconut trees in the Pampa region of Argentina as well as beds of seashells at the foot of the eastern side of the Andes Mountains. This suggested that the entire lowlands of Argentina were once underwater. He discovered that the mighty Amazon River had a very small delta and the Orinoco River, a much smaller river in Northern Venezuela, had a very large delta. Certainly, the size of a river's delta can designate the age of the river. This physical evidence along with the breakthrough evidence at the Obidos Narrows led him to theorize that the great Amazon River basin was once an inland sea, and that only recently did the Amazon Basin drain, and the river flow to the Atlantic along its current path.

There is also evidence to suggest that the lower part of the Isthmus of Darien was as well under water at one time, and that there was no land bridge between South America and Central America. There are no Pre-Columbian ruins at all in Panama. New geological evidence suggests that Panama is the newest significant land mass on the earth's crust to rise out of the ocean. Its connection of the continents of North and South America altered the flow of the oceans and changed the patterns of weather significantly. What could have happened to change the face of the land so much? Many geologists and scientists have studied the Andean Mountain ranges through the years. There is good evidence that a chain eruption of volcanoes along the Andean Cordillera could have been responsible for the whole surface of the continental plate being lifted up 200 feet in some places to as much as 3400 feet in other places which brought much of Argentina, Uruguay, Paraguay, and Brazil up above the water line. This kind of horrific natural phenomenon would account for such catastrophic changes in the earth's surface that would be described in the Book of Mormon at the time of Christ as: "**the whole face of the land changed**".

Venice Priddis's account of this upheaval in her book, *The Book and the Map* is quite good. She describes how this Andean Highland area was once an island and then at the time of Christ great destruction and upheaval caused by earthquakes and then corresponding volcanic eruptions caused the whole land mass of South America is rise up out of the sea and evolve into the continent we know now as South America. **The whole Face of the Land Changed…..**

"For behold, the whole face of the land was changed, because of the tempest and the whirlwinds and the thunderings and the

Figure #11 Map of present day South America

lightnings, and the exceeding great quaking of the whole earth." (3 Nephi 8:11-15).

The language of this scripture would indicate that catastrophic changes in the 'face of the land' took place along the entire length of the Nephite Island from Colombia to the tip of Chile. Geological evidences such as

Figure #12 A map of the South American continent before the time of Christ.

82   BOOK OF MORMON GEOGRAPHY

the heaving upward of lower Chile from the ocean's bottom, the rising of Tiahuanaco to about 3,400 feet above its previous level, and the possible rising of the 150-mile 'Darien Gap' at Panama show this to be true. Apparently all the geological changes took place within the space of three hours. (3 Nephi 8:19.)

19. "And it came to pass that when the thunderings, and the lightnings, and the storm, and the tempest, and the quakings of the earth did cease – for behold, they did last for about the space of three hours; and it was said by some that the time was greater; nevertheless, all these great and terrible things were done in about the space of three hours – and then behold, there was darkness upon the face of the land." (3 Nephi 8:19.)

Volcanic eruptions along the so-called 'fire-lane,' which stretches along the entire length of the Andes Mountains, could easily have been the means the Lord used to effect these changes. There are 212 known volcanoes in this fire lane of the Andes; some of them are still active today. Chain-reaction volcanic activity is not an uncommon thing along the fire-lane. Charles Darwin, himself, tells of seeing the volcano Osorno erupt while

Picture #12
This is one of the many volcanic mountain peaks in the Andean 'Fire Lane'.

he stood on the deck of the Beagle. The erupting volcano was about forty miles inland. Darwin was surprised to hear afterwards that the Aconcagua another volcano located about 480 miles northward of Osorno, had also erupted. He was even more surprised when he heard that the volcano Coseguina, about 2,700 miles north of the volcano Aconcagua, had erupted, causing a great earthquake which was felt within a thousand-mile radius. The Coseguina erupted within six hours of the others. According to his report, volcanic activity can, and sometimes does, take place almost simultaneously along this fire-lane belt.

Volcanic action could have given rise not only to the earthquakes and avalanches (3 Nephi 9:5) but also to the tempests, including hail, strong winds, and rain (3 Nephi 8:12), lightning, thunder, whirlwinds and tornadoes (3 Nephi 8:12, 16), and fire and hot lava (3 Nephi 9:11). Frank W. Lane said that weather in the immediate area of a volcano is largely created by the effects of the eruption. "In all violent eruptions there are thunderstorms with brilliant lightning, hail, and heavy rains." The great heat in some eruptions also caused tornadoes. For example: "During the great eruption of Tambora [Indonesia] in April 1815, the most violent tornadoes formed. They snatched up men, horses, cattle, and anything movable. The largest trees were torn out of the ground by the roots and whirled into the air". Ref 11. This too is consistent with the Book of Mormon account, wherein we read: "And there were some who were carried away in the whirlwind; and whither they went no man knoweth…." (3 Nephi 8:16.)

Priddis theorizes that: "The upheavals around Zarahemla and Bountiful would have been very great, but in the land northward they must have been of tremendous magnitude." The records say, "…there was a more great and terrible destruction in the land northward….." (3 Nephi 8:12.) There are about twenty-two very high peaks in Ecuador. With so many volcanoes, Mt. Chimborazo could have erupted, along with several others in that area leaving the land scorched and burned, trees uprooted, some cities flattened and some buried beneath tons of lava and volcanic ash.

…..Charles Darwin claimed that the Andes, along the lower half of Chile, had been raised in a very recent period, geologically speaking. R.T. Chamberlin tells us that when the Andes rose in South America," hundreds, if not thousands, of cubic miles of the body of the earth almost instantaneously heaved upward [producing] a violent earthquake which spread….throughout the entire globe."

After three hours the quaking and tempests stopped. (3 Nephi 8:19.) Thick darkness settled over the land, presumably in the form of ash and dust clouds; a darkness which lasted three days. (3 Nephi 8:23.) Following the eruption of Tambora, Indonesia (April 1815), "a vast dust cloud turned day into night for hundreds of miles around the volcano, darkness....lasted for three days…. The same thing was true at Maura 310 miles away.

While there was tremendous destruction, the sites of some cities remained unchanged. For instance, Zarahemla, burned but was later rebuilt. Other cities and lands were also restored. (4 Nephi 7-8.) Apparently the Sidon River still flowed much as it had before the catastrophe. (Mormon 1:10.)" Ref 11.

On May 18, 1980 when Mt. St. Helens had its volcanic eruption the weather conditions were very similar to the account in the Book of Mormon. The tremendous amount of ash lingered in the air for three hundred miles around, for a period of three days. Helicopters, trucks, any motorized vehicles could not be used, breathing air had to be used for rescues, etc. The sky was dark at mid morning and visibility was only a few feet.

> 20 "And it came to pass that there was thick darkness upon all the face of the land, insomuch that the inhabitants thereof who had not fallen could feel the vapour of darkness;
>
> 21 And there could be no light, because of the darkness, neither candles, neither torches; neither could there be fire kindled with their fine and exceedingly dry wood, so that there could not be any light at all;
>
> 22 And there was not any light seen, neither fire, nor glimmer, neither the sun, nor the moon, nor the stars, for so great were the mists of darkness which were upon the face of the land.
>
> 23 And it came to pass that it did last for the space of three days that there was no light seen; and there was great mourning and howling and weeping among all the people continually; yea, great were the groanings of the people, because of the darkness and the great destruction which had come upon them." 3 Nephi 8:20-23

The USGS Cascades Volcano Observatory report states that the volcano was triggered by an earthquake of 5.1 magnitude a mile beneath the volcano. The ash fallout was detectable in 22,000 square miles and the ash depth was 10 inches at 10 miles downwind, one inch at 60 miles downwind, and ½ inch at 300 miles downwind, it spread clear across the U.S. in three days. If this phenomenon is magnified by several volcanoes erupting at once in a chain reaction, the destruction to the whole area would have been incredible and changed forever the face of the land.

ISLES OF THE SEA

South America before Christ was probably quite a bit smaller, an island, really that consisted mostly of the Andean highlands. See the adjoining map of the continent of South America before the time of Christ and our proposed 'Isle of the Sea'. After they arrived at the 'Promised Land', Nephi and Jacob continually preached and prophesied about being on an island and sited many times the prophecies and the blessings to the people from the isles of the sea from Zenos and Isaiah. References to 'Isles of the sea' occurs at least ten times in the books of 1st Nephi, 2nd Nephi, and Jacob. Jacob says:

> "20.....nevertheless, we have been driven out of the land of our inheritance; but we have been led to a better land, for the Lord has made the sea our path, and we are upon an **isle of the sea**.
>
> 21. But great are the promises of the Lord unto them who are upon the **isles of the sea**; wherefore as it says **isles**, there must needs be more than this, and they are inhabited also by our brethren." 2Nephi 10:20-21

Our theories postulate that South America was once this very 'Island of the Sea' that Jacob and others prophesied about before the land was changed. Ref 11. Obviously, when Lehi and his family first landed they could not have done enough exploring to ascertain for sure that they were indeed on an island. The interesting thing is that in the Book of Mormon after the time of Christ no mention of their homeland being an 'island' is ever made again. The only association of an 'island' with the 'Promised Land' occurs before the time of Christ.

South America would still have been over 3000 miles long and average several hundred miles wide before the time of Christ. Only at the Gulf of Guayaquil in Ecuador does the island shrink to 50 to 70 miles in width, which becomes our narrow neck of land spoken of. Probably the reason that they knew about their island home was because Lehi had seen in vision the 'Promised Land' as it had been shown to him by the Lord. (1Nephi 5:5.) Also, Nephi makes reference to seeing the 'Promised Land' in a vision as well.

> "And it came to pass that the angel said unto me: Look, and behold thy seed, and also the seed of thy brethren. And I looked and beheld multitudes of people, yea, even as it were in number as many; as the sand of the sea. (1Nephi 12:1)

Both of these early Book of Mormon prophets saw the 'Land of Promise' in vision before they actually arrived on its shores.

On a vacation trip to New Zealand we asked our native tour guide where the Maori people originated and he gave us the standard historical answer of the Easter Islands. On further promptings about where the Maori legends say the people came from he finally stated, "My ancestors speak of coming forth from the 'long island' in the beginning of our traditions which was the 'mother of our civilization'." This is very interesting since the period of the migrations and Hagoth spoken of in the Book of Mormon occurred around 70 B.C. before the land changed, and when the mother civilization would still have been a long narrow island.

SOUTH AMERICA BEFORE CHRIST
THE LAND

The continent of South America before the time of Christ then would have been considerably different than the way it looks today. The 'Promised Land' spoken of in the scriptures would have to be today a mountainous land full of volcanoes, mountains, rivers, and valleys to satisfy all the descriptions in the Book of Mormon. It would be a land full of Pre-Columbian ruins that survived the tremendous upheavals after Jesus Christ, where the whole face of the land changed. The Andean Highlands is the only area in the New World which can completely satisfy all of these parameters set out in our study. A proposed map of the continent on the next page shows that South America is just a relatively small area (compared to the Continent as it is today) consisting primarily of the Andean Mountain chain, with a northern area and a southern area and a small neck of land in between. This island chain consisted mainly of three types of land areas: the coastal deserts, mountains, and mountain valleys or highlands.

The Andean Mountain valleys then had beautiful rich fertile soil as they still have today. These valleys are the ancestral home of the sweet potato, potato, corn, maize, peanut, tomato, and so many other crops. To this day the native Quechua people still grow hundreds of different varieties of corn and potatoes. In the various migrations, Lehi's family (1 Nephi 8:1), the Jaredites (Ether 2:3) and Mulekites, also brought with them from the Old World seeds of many varieties. The soil is a reddish brown loam soil that is naturally very fertile and easily tillable. Using a combination of natural rainfall during the rainy season and irrigation from the plentiful springs and rivers, these valleys were very productive. It is not hard to imagine the yearning of Nephi and his group to leave the hot, parched, and arid areas near the coastline for the more fertile and better climates of the mountain valleys. These Andean Mountain valleys have a nice cool climate, nice sunny warm days, and very long growing periods for long season crops such as potatoes, tomatoes, corn, and squash.

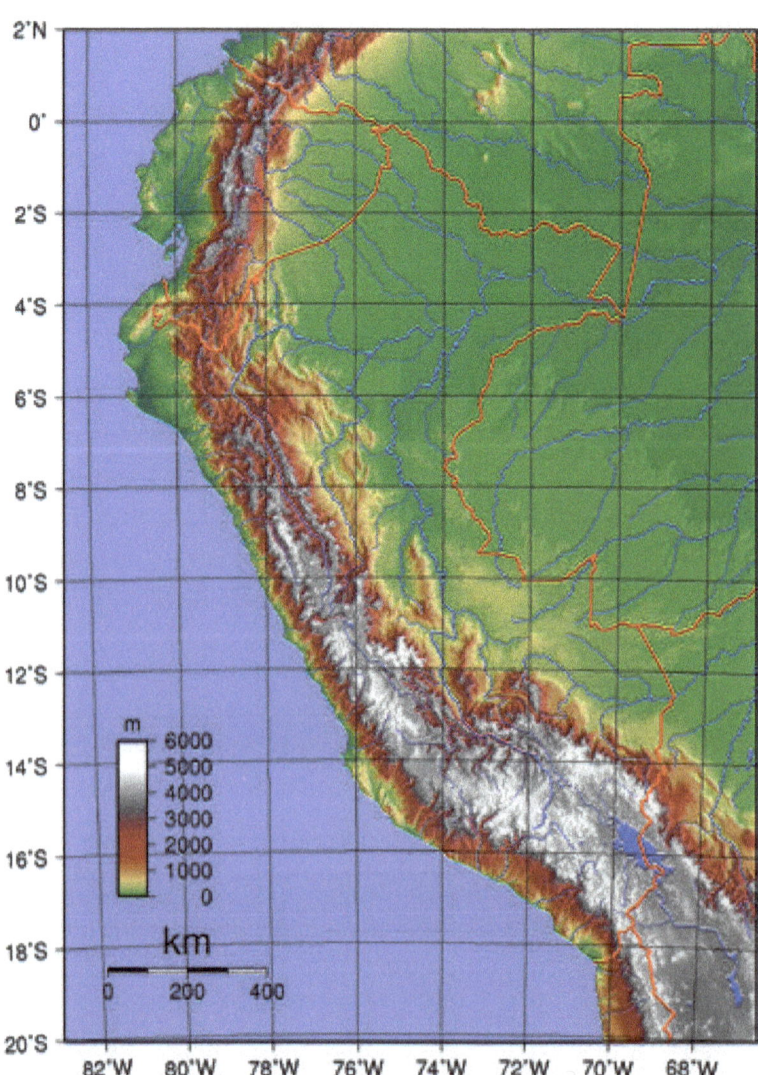

Figure #13 Map of Andean Mountain range in South America.

THE MENTAL IMAGE

It is important that every reader of the Book of Mormon have a mental image of the 'Promised Land' at this point. The spatial configuration that we have been building should look somewhat like this following diagram:

Lehi's landing in the south would be the southern most point because the only direction that the Book of Mormon takes from their landing and their land of their 'first inheritance' is always north. The whole area is an island, with a land to the north and a land to the south with a narrow neck of land placed in between. We will learn more about the narrow neck of land later. We can start placing in our mind other features into our diagram as we go further and build on the image. As we read the Book of Mormon we can for example start placing other facts that we know about on our mental image map like the City of Nephi. We know that Nephi took his group 'many days' journey to the north into the interior of this island but not northerly enough to come to the narrow neck of land. Similarly, we can start placing other features such as wilderness areas, prominent cities, and places, as we read and study the Book of Mormon. It is a natural thing that everyone that intently studies the Book of Mormon draws for themselves a mental picture of the book's geography in their minds as they read and progress through the book. One of the purposes of this work is to help guide a person with his or her mental picture and to make the whole process more exciting and pleasurable.

THE INCAN ROADS

The Incas are famous for their road building throughout their history. The Spanish conquistadors were amazed at the road construction that they found carved out of the mountains and into the jungles when they arrived in Peru. An intricate road system connected the empire from sea level to high into the snow covered Andean mountains and from Chile to northern Colombia some three thousand miles in length. See the following map of ancient Incan roads that are still known to modern times.

THE CLIMATE

The Andean Highland climate is always cool and humid year round. It has exceptional growing conditions: a mild climate with an average daytime temperature of 18 degrees Celsius (65' F), a rich flora and fauna, fertile soil, and many streams. The growing season was year round, but consisted of a wet season and a dry season. Being fairly close to the equator, they relied heavily upon the sun's shadows on their monolithic sundials to determine

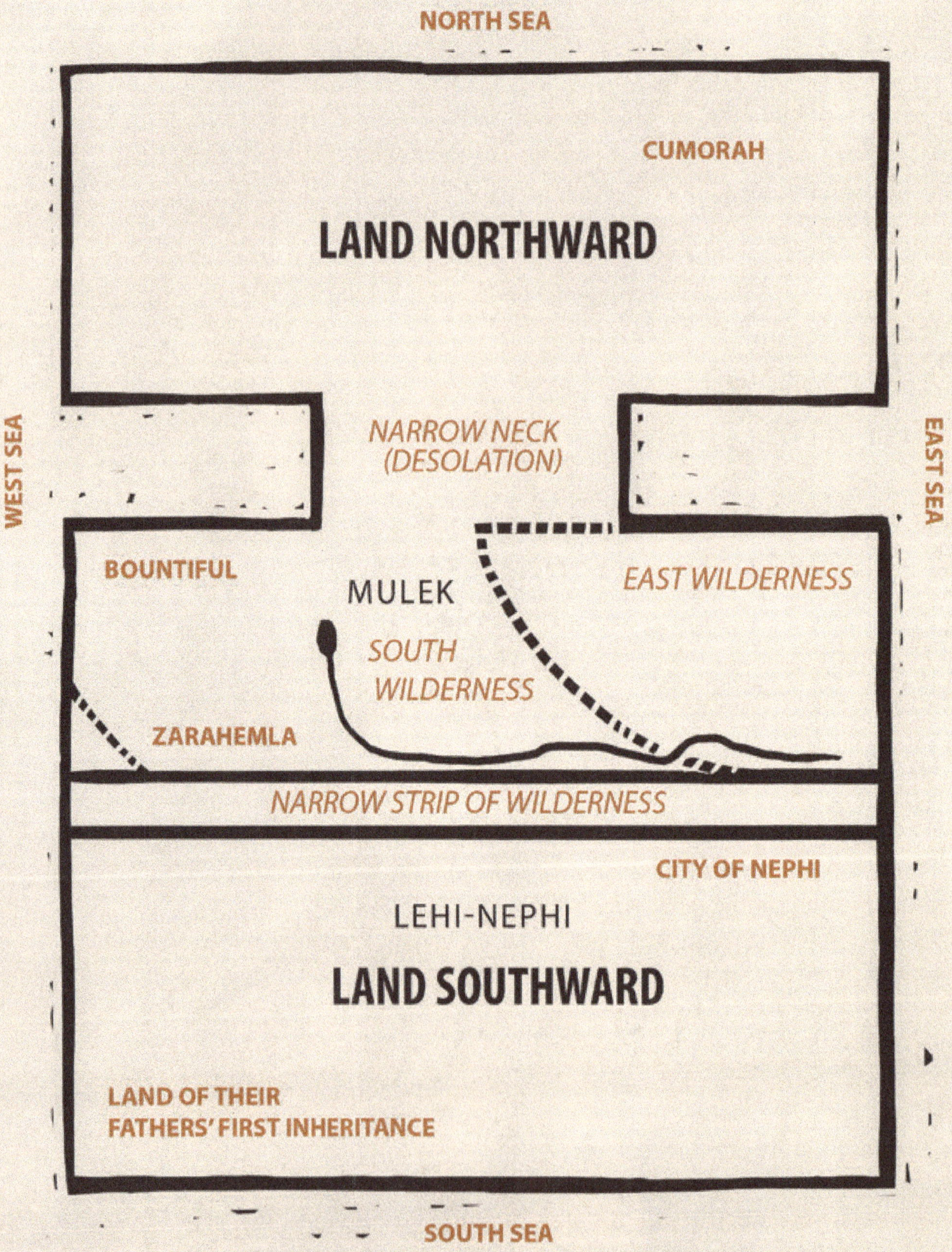

NORTH SEA

CUMORAH

LAND NORTHWARD

WEST SEA

NARROW NECK
(DESOLATION)

EAST SEA

BOUNTIFUL

MULEK

EAST WILDERNESS

*SOUTH
WILDERNESS*

ZARAHEMLA

NARROW STRIP OF WILDERNESS

CITY OF NEPHI

LEHI-NEPHI

LAND SOUTHWARD

LAND OF THEIR
FATHERS' FIRST INHERITANCE

SOUTH SEA

GENERIC SPATIAL CONFIGURATION

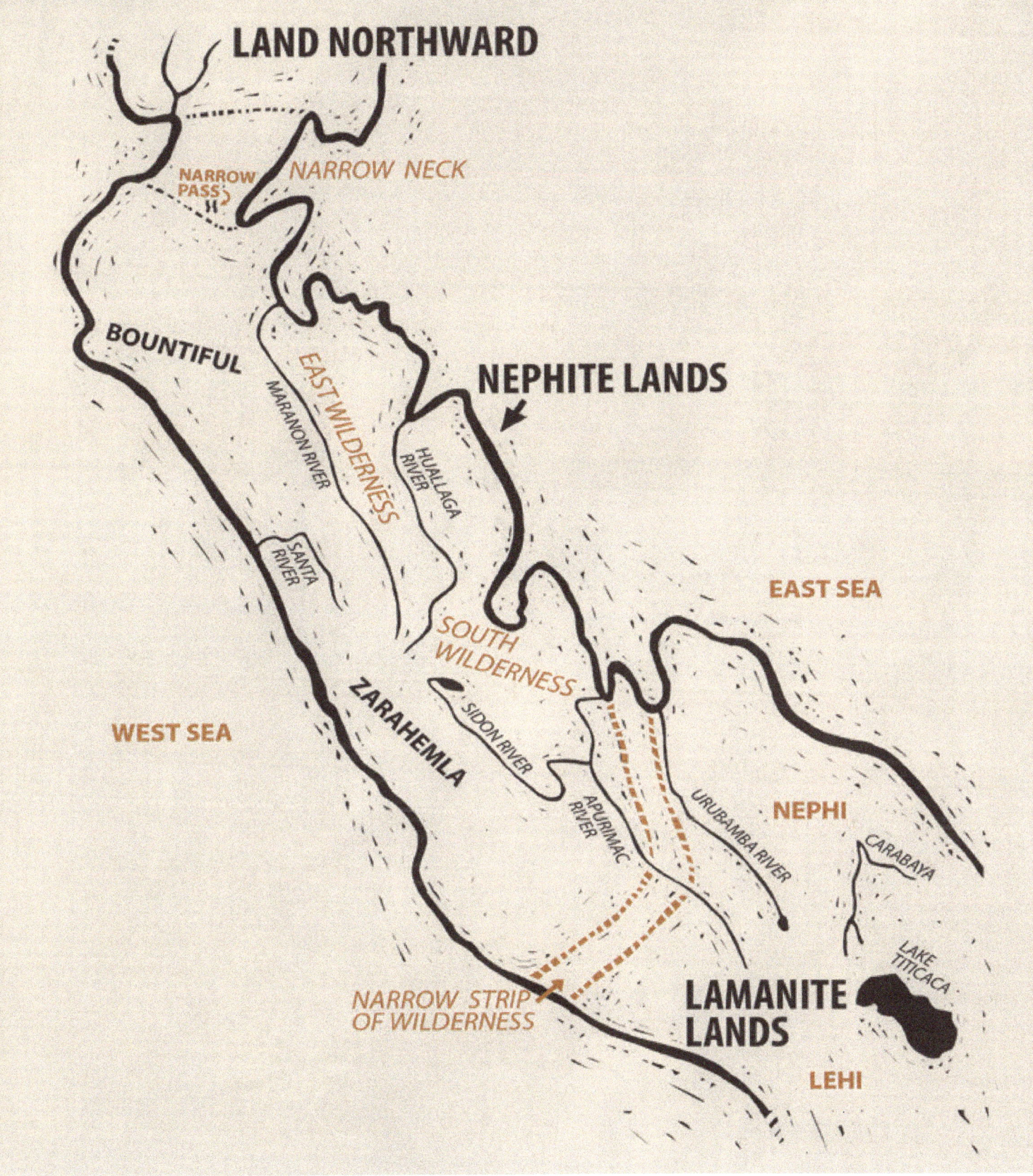

Figure #15 This map shows the Nephite lands that connected all of their important city locations and also the location of the narrow neck of the land.

Figure #14 Basic mental image or visual concept of the geography for the average reader of the Book of Mormon.

THE CITY OF NEPHI

the subtle change in the length of the day to determine the day of the year. This was very important to know when to plant and when the rains would come. The coastal climate was much different than the highlands. It was very hot and dry desert conditions, as it is even today. In some coastal areas it was so dry that it never rained for years at a time. Population in these regions even today are only sustained by the flow of rivers from the high Andes Mountains that flow down to the Pacific Ocean. Before the land changed the mountain valley highland elevation was most likely lower which would have created an even milder climate than what they have today.

Picture #13a
The llama was a domesticated member of the cameloid family.

THE ANIMALS

Also, a real advantage is the lack of bugs, snakes, and other undesirable animals because of the high altitude. The people over time found several types of animals that were acclimatized well to the area. The llama, alpaca, vicuna, guinea pig, became useful animals and were domesticated. One of the criteria for an ancient civilization is that it has time to domesticate different wild animal species native to the country. The llama and the guinea pig were definitely domesticated by these Pre-Inca peoples. The natives of Mexico and Central America on the other hand are younger civilizations because they did not have time to domesticate the native wild

Picture #13b
A picture of a group of wild Vicunas. A smaller cameloid whose fur was the most highly prized and could only be worn by Incan Royalty.

THE CITY OF NEPHI 93

animals in their homelands. These species along with herds of sheep, pigs, cattle, horses, donkeys, and goats were common in the mountain valleys.

> 25. And it came to pass that we did find upon the land of promise, as we journeyed in the wilderness, that there were beasts in the forests of every kind, both the cow and the ox, and the ass and the horse, and the goat and the wild goat, and all manner of wild animals, which were for the use of men. And we did find all manner of ore, both of gold, and of silver, and of copper. 1Nephi 18:25

Critics of the Book of Mormon have for a long time objected to this verse in the record, because supposedly the horse and other animals mentioned were not found in the Americas before the Spanish conquests. However, this has proven to be false with discoveries of pre-historic skeletons of horses found in the La Brea Tar Pits of Los Angeles, California that pre-date the Spanish by hundreds of years.

> "On February 18, 2009, George C. Page Museum formally announced the 2006 discovery of 16 fossil deposits which had been removed from the ground during the construction of an underground parking garage for the Los Angeles County Museum of Art next to the tar pits. Among the finds are remains of a saber-toothed cat, six dire wolves, **bison, horses,** a giant ground sloth, turtles, snails, clams, millipedes, fish, gophers, and an American lion. Also discovered is a nearly intact **mammoth** skeleton, nicknamed Zed; the only pieces missing are a rear leg, a vertebra and the top of its skull, which was sheared off by construction equipment in preparation to build the parking structure." Ref. 32

So, an analysis of the Book of Mormon would also suggest that Nephi and his party found these animals in the forests as they traveled along the way in the wilderness. They were not found on the arid coast and the area of their first inheritance. This is further suggesting, that they were not animals that they brought with them from Jerusalem to the Promised Land, but that they were already in the Promised Land. Many times the writers in the Book of Mormon reference the flocks and herds that the Nephites were raising. So, where did this great diversity of animals originate? Were they all native to the Americas and leftover from the Creation and the Garden of Eden? We may never know completely, but the Book of Mormon does give us other clues from the Book of Ether and the Jaredite civilization about 2200 B.C. The Lord commanded the brother of Jared to prepare themselves and to gather their flocks for their journey to a 'Choice Land'.

> 41. "Go to and gather together thy **flocks, both male and female, of every kind**; and also of the seed of the earth of every kind; and thy families; and also Jared thy brother and his family; and also thy friends and their families, and the friends of Jared and their families." Ether 1:41

This would account for many of the domestic farm animals that were brought to the Americas if the land needed to be repopulated after the great flood. The Jaredites also brought with them wild animals and fish.

> 2. "And they did also lay snares and catch fowls of the air; and they did also prepare a vessel, in which they did carry with them the fish of the waters." Ether 2:2

Later, in Ether, after many centuries of growth the record gives a status of these animals that have been nurtured in the Americas:

> 17. "Having all manner of fruit, and of grain, and of silks, and of fine linen, and of gold, and of silver, and of precious things;
>
> 18. And also all manner of **cattle, of oxen, and cows, and of sheep, and of swine, and of goats,** and also many other kinds of animals which were useful for the food of man.
>
> 19. And they also had **horses, and asses, and there were elephants** and cureloms and cumoms; all of which were useful unto man, and more especially the **elephants** and cureloms and cumoms." Ether 9:17-19

It shouldn't surprise a student of the Book of Mormon that there were a huge number of certain types of animals when the Spanish arrive and a lack of other animals mentioned; because we know of the devastating wars and the scorched earth polices and the extermination of the herds by the Lamanites and the Gadianton Robbers from the scriptures. It becomes apparent that not all of these animals and herds survived to the modern era when the Spanish Chroniclers began their recordings.

THE CROPS

The first activity that the Children of Lehi did when they reached the 'Land Bountiful' was to put their seeds into the ground and raise crops. We assume several different grain crops because that is what is mentioned mostly, but these crops could have also included various vegetables as well. Again, when they first arrived in the 'Promised Land' their first labor was to sow their seeds and tend their crops. And again, when they arrived in the 'Land of Nephi' their first priority was to plant their crops

Picture #14
Peruvian man dyeing wool for weaving purposes.

96 BOOK OF MORMON GEOGRAPHY

to feed themselves. Similarly, the Jaredites recorded the same priority of planting their crops as their first activity in their new land. Coming from an arid to moderate climate in the Near East and Mediterranean area then we assume for their seeds to be successful they would have had to have a similar climate and growing conditions. Therefore, the Chilean coastline and equatorial climate of Peru would have been an area where these crops would have flourished and responded with excellent results. Peru is home to a wide variety of crops, many of which are deemed to be native to Peru including: corn, sweet potatoes, potatoes, tomatoes, squash, beans, and all manner of grains.

Even though the land changed immensely, these mountain valleys probably have not changed much from the beginning of time. Crops grown today still flourish abundantly as they did before the 'Land Changed'. The Cusco and Andean Highlands produce an amazing abundance of agricultural crops that are the basis of life for the native people of this area. The forces of nature may have elevated these regions some in altitude which would have had the effect of slightly cooler temperatures; but it is unlikely that this would have changed the climate too radically. Life in these mountain valleys at 10,000 to 12,000 feet above sea level is about the same today as it probably existed in 590 B.C. when Nephi first inhabited these remote lands.

THE HONEY BEE – DESERET

When the Jaredites crossed the ocean to the Americas in 2200 B.C. they brought Deseret or the Honey Bee with them in their sealed up boats. The duration of the voyage could have been nearly a whole year. So, that would have been quite a problem if humans were sealed up in the same small space as the honey bees for the whole trip. The native honey bee in South America (Meliponids) is a stingless variety that only lives in tropical areas, such as the Middle East, Asia, parts of Africa, and Central and South America. This variety of honey bee is smaller and less productive than the commercial hybrid varieties from Europe nowadays, but it was completely harmless because it was stingless. Apparently, there are no native honey bees in North America, all bee varieties have been imported. So, the theory is that this stingless honey bee would have been easy to transport to the 'Promised Land', and therefore would have been very useful to their society and their agricultural way of life.

3. "And they did also carry with them deseret, which, by interpretation, is a honey bee; and thus they did carry with them swarms of bees, and all manner of that which was upon the face of the land, seeds of every kind." Ether 1:3

THE PEOPLE

The two groups, Nephites and Lamanites were considerably different in their approach to feed and clothe themselves. From the very beginning of their sojourn in this new 'Promised Land' each group's attitude was the reflection of their leader's traits, attributes, and goals. Each of their life styles led to particular research criteria that have completely separated the two races over the centuries that we will now discuss.

Early Nephites

Nephi was physically large in stature. His progeny most likely could be classified as exceedingly beautiful, white and delightsome as the scriptures describe them, and as an unusually large race of people, dictated by his genetics. This stature combined with their dedicated faith gave them much strength in battle even against overwhelming odds. Nephi and his group were ambitious and diligent farmers. Nephi says," ….and I did teach my people to plant crops and till the earth….1Nephi 18:24 & 2Nephi 5:11. There is not an area in Pre-Columbian ruins where agricultural reserves, experiment stations, terraces, and waterways are in more evidence than here in the Andean Highlands. An example of this inspired leadership is an incredible agricultural experiment station with fantastic terraces and irrigation canals built at different elevations to test the performance of crop varieties at Malady near Cusco, Peru.

Another famous Pre-Inca agricultural reserve exists at Mara, which is close to Cusco as well. This incredible set of ruins is built in circular patterns that involve changes in several hundred feet of elevation, and incredible experimental agricultural facility. These farming operations obviously took centuries to build and develop, but the groundwork and concepts were no doubt developed early, possibly by Nephi and his small group.

The amazing hillside terraces of Peru are all irrigated by means of stone water pipelines or canals that bring fresh water from springs or streams sometimes many miles away. The population of the Andean Highlands is said to have peaked at around fifteen million people which could only have been supported by intense cultivation of these hillside terraced lands. The early Nephites were taught to build buildings, till the earth, and animal husbandry. Nephi taught his people to read and write their language. He also made weapons of war, and taught his people how to use them. The museums are full of examples of fine gold, bronze, and copper metallurgy. The artefacts in these museums testify that Nephi did teach his people the art of metallurgy, the making of weapons of war, and fine twined linen. The ancient Incas were world renown for their textiles and weaving. Many examples of their magnificent work can be witnessed in today's museums.

Picture #15
Pre-Inca agricultural reserve at Mara in its restored condition.

About 179 years after Lehi left Jerusalem, the prophet Enos gives this description of the Nephite people and how they were doing in the Land of Nephi:

> 21. "And it came to pass that the people of Nephi did till the land, and raise all manner of grain, and of fruit, and flocks of herds, and flocks of all manner of cattle of every kind, and goats, and wild goats, and also many horses.
>
> 22. And there were exceedingly many prophets among us. And the people were a stiffnecked people, hard to understand."
> Enos 1:21-22

The Nephites were very industrious and worked hard to prosper in the land and to obtain their possessions. The Lamanites for the most part were completely opposite and were lazy and coveted the lands and possessions of the Nephites.

Early Lamanites

Nephi describes the Lamanites in his narrative written on the golden plates this way:

> 20. Wherefore, the word of the Lord was fulfilled which he spake unto me, saying that: inasmuch as they will not hearken unto thy words they shall be cut off from the presence of the Lord. And behold they were cut off from his presence.
>
> 21. And he had caused the cursing to come upon them, yea even a sore cursing, because of their iniquity. For behold, they had hardened their hearts against him, that they had become like unto flint; wherefore, as they were white, and exceedingly fair and delightsome, that they might not be enticing unto my people the Lord God did cause a skin of blackness to come upon them.
>
> 22. And thus saith the Lord God: I will cause that they shall be loathsome unto thy people, save they shall repent of their iniquities.
>
> 23. And cursed shall be the seed of him that mixeth with their seed; for they shall be cursed even with the same cursing. And the Lord spake it, and it was done.

24. And because of their cursing which was upon them they did become an idle people, full of mischief and subtlety, and did seek in the wilderness for beasts of prey. 2Nephi 5:20-24

The Lamanites according to this scripture were a dark skinned people, and most likely shorter in stature and less fair than the Nephites.

Picture #16
A native woman weaves a blanket using traditional llama wool.

These people, the Lamanites, on the other hand were strictly hunters and gatherers. They were a lazy and idolatrous people. Mosiah 9:12. There is no doubt that the reason the Lamanites followed and battled the Nephites wasn't just to get the Brass Plates back. They also wanted the land and the improvements that Nephi and his group had struggled and worked hard to obtain and maintain. Basically, the Lamanite people were very nomadic even though they apparently did eventually build several cities. They were more content in their history to rob and plunder and battle the Nephites to be able to steal their possessions. The prophet Enos writes about the Lamanites:

> 20. "And I bear record that the people of Nephi did seek diligently to restore the Lamanites unto the true faith in God. But our labours were vain; their hatred was fixed, and they were led by their evil nature that they became wild, and ferocious, and a blood-thirsty people, full of idolatry and filthiness; feeding upon beasts of prey; dwelling in tents, and wandering about in the wilderness with a short skin girdle about their loins and their heads shaven; and their skill was in the bow, and in the cimeter, and the ax. And many of them did eat nothing save it was raw meat; and they were continually seeking to destroy us." Enos 1:20

The Lamanites were at times going to battle with very little armament or clothing. And Alma 3:5 says that they only wore a loin cloth about themselves. The Andean Mountain valleys can be quite cool at times and wet during the rainy season which suggests that the climate could have been a bit warmer and dryer during this time period than it is now. However, if the actual altitude was somewhat lower before the time of Christ, then that would also account for the warmer, dryer conditions. But still going around almost naked at sea level in the dry desert conditions of the coastal regions of their 'first inheritance' wouldn't have been as uncomfortable as the Andean Altiplano. The Nephite writers no doubt mentioned the Lamanites's lack of clothing and armour because of the natural cool climatic conditions of their land before the time of Christ. They were amazed at how little clothing the Lamanites wore into battle.

NARROW NECK OF LAND

One of the most important spatial aspects of the geography of the Book of Mormon is the 'Narrow Neck of Land' that is so often talked about. The 'Narrow Neck of Land' separated the 'land North from the land South' with the 'Sea East' only a day and a half journey from the 'Sea West' Alma 50:34. This narrow neck of land is the defining attribute of the Book of Mormon lands.

"And now, it was only the distance of a day and a half's journey for a Nephite, on the line Bountiful and the land Desolation, from the east to the west sea; and thus the land of Nephi and the land of Zarahemla were nearly surrounded by water, there being a small neck of land between the land northward and the land southward." Alma 22:32.

Everyone at first glance is prone to assume that the narrow neck of land spoken of would be Panama or the Isthmus of Darien. The other obvious choice would be the Isthmus of Tehuantepec in Honduras. But on closer study both isthmuses do not conform to the pattern spoken of in the Book of Mormon. There is no land Northward or Southward or 'East Sea' and 'West Sea' looking at the map in Figure #16.

Figure #16 Map of non-qualifying isthmuses or narrow necks of land.

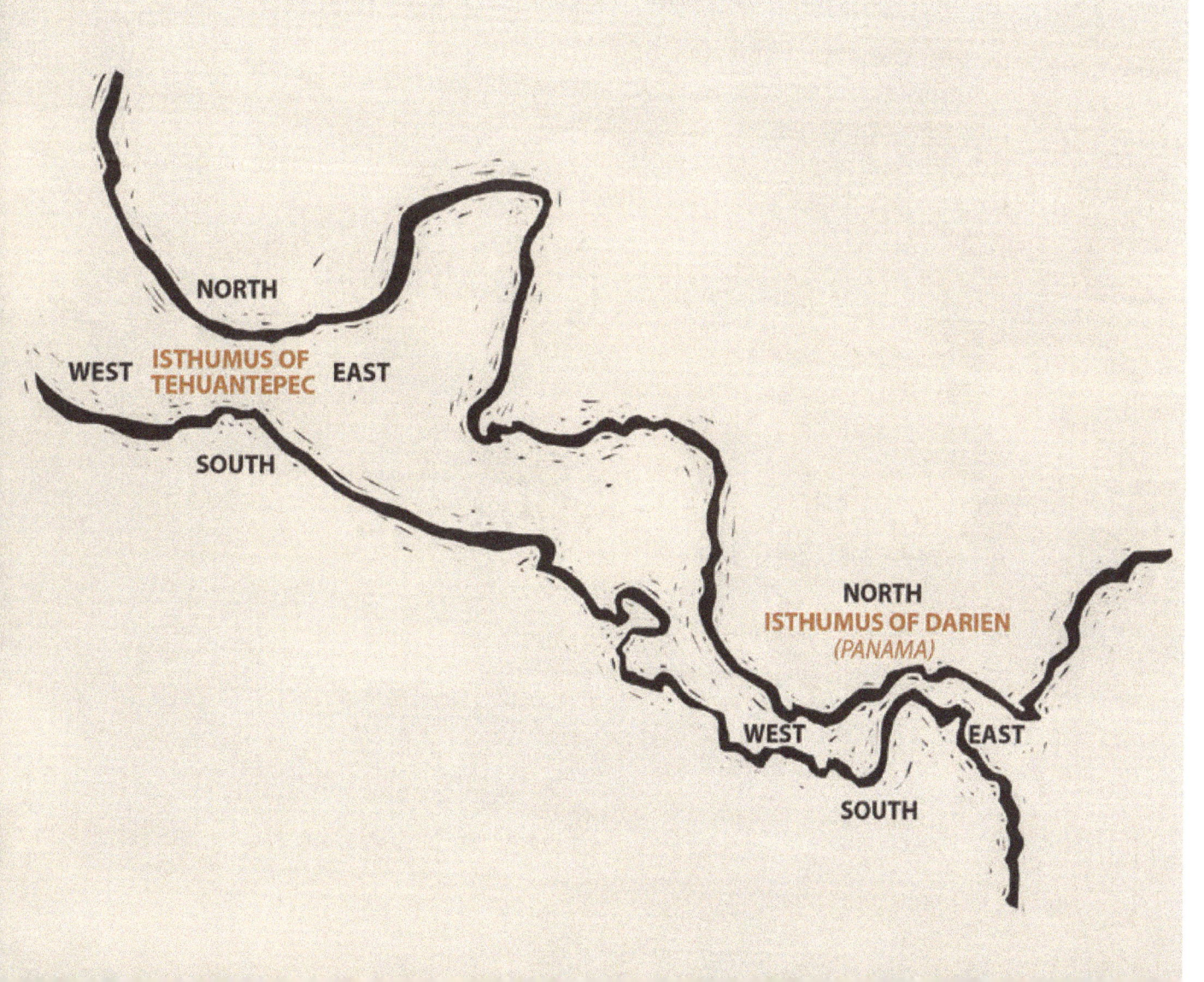

The land mass configuration would have to be turned a full 90° to meet the Book of Mormon requirement. The Nephites were such great astronomers as evidenced by ruins all over the Americas it is hard to imagine that they could be out 90° in their compass reading. Using the sun and the stars for their orientation they would never be wrong regarding the 'Sea East' and the 'Sea West' as an example. Also, as Priddis pointed out in her book, *The Book and the Map* there are no ruins even close to Panama and the Isthmus of Tehuantepec in Honduras is really too wide to be a day and a half's journey for a Nephite. Ref 11.

Again focusing on South America and our little island chain of the Andean Region we finally see the proper narrow neck of land spoken of in the Book of Mormon. The Gulf of Guayaquil in Ecuador is a natural break in the coastal line of the Pacific. When we truly focus our attention on South America as being the 'Promised Land' of Lehi, then we discover our narrow neck of land at the Gulf of Guayaquil in Ecuador. We now resolve one of the great stumbling blocks of the Book of Mormon geography. In fact looking at our proposed map (Map #3) of South America before the land changed, it can be seen that this narrow neck satisfies all the criteria talked about in the scriptures. There is a 'Sea East' and a 'Sea West' and a 'land Northward and a land Southward'. From Loja and the Zamora River to the 'Sea West', the Gulf of Guayaquil it is only 75 miles. Also, another feature of the narrow neck of land was that it had to have a narrow pass associated with it. (Alma 50:34; 52:9 and Mormon 2:29; 3:5) This narrow pass also existed after the land changed and is seen today in modern times.

Priddis says, "North of Loja and south of Saraguro there is a high and narrow pass called 'El Paso del Oro,' (The Golden Pass or The Golden Way). It is an important pass, one which in early days had a way of controlling movement between Peru and Ecuador. In the days of the conquistadores, a battle called 'La Batalla del Oro' was fought to conquer that pass. When we recognize the location of this pass in connection with the narrow neck of land it is easy to see why the two terms have been used synonymously." Ref 11. This area all along the west coast of South America and Central America is the only place that strictly conforms to all the requirements set up in Alma 22:32 regarding the narrow neck of land before the time of Christ and before the whole face of the land was changed.

> "And now, it was only the distance of a day and a half's journey for a Nephite, on the line Bountiful and the Land of Desolation, from the east to the west sea; and thus the land

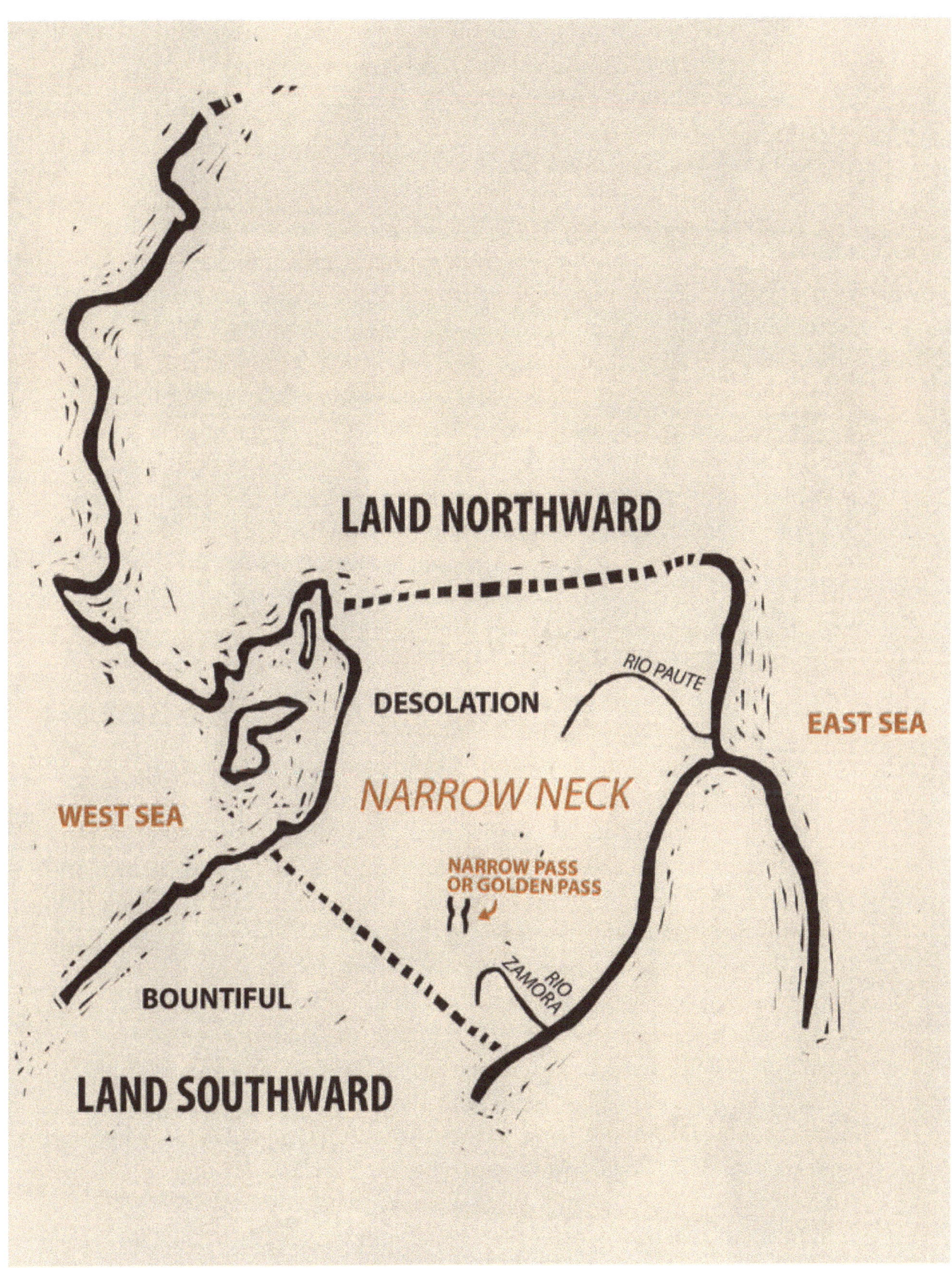

Figure #17 A more complete map of the narrow neck of land with its narrow pass.

of Nephi and the land of Zarahemla were nearly surrounded by water, there being a small neck of land between the land northward and the land southward. Alma 22:32

SOUTH AMERICA AFTER CHRIST

Today the continent of South America is not a small island of the sea, but it is a major land mass with a cosmopolitan population of millions of people that have immigrated here from many countries in search of freedom and a new way of life. South America is a continent with many countries and it appears so completely different today from what it was before the time of Christ and before the 'whole face of the land changed'.

In the Andean Highland today life continues much the same as it has for the centuries since the time of Christ. The agrarian lifestyle continues to sustain the masses. Modern innovations have come to the mountain valleys with the tractor, cultivator, and disc, but the native farmer can still be seen turning the soil with a foot plough as well. Modern cities dot the land with their hotels, businesses, and highways. Cars, trucks, and buses transport the people and their goods, but if you look closely you can still see the ancient Inca roads, the llamas, and their beautiful pre-Columbian stonework.

The various countries of South America enjoy more religious and political freedom and prosperity today than ever before in modern history. That freedom from Colonial Spanish and Portuguese rule and the inquisition period started in the 1820's and coincided with the restoration of the Gospel. Jose San Martin, Simon Bolivar, and others were the liberation heroes of the 1820's in South America. Both generals were Masons and had many of the same attributes of the American Founding Fathers. They were the liberators of this land that brought more freedom than ever before in their history and eventually paved the way for the gospel to be preached here in our modern day. The LDS Church population is exploding in these countries today in fulfillment of prophecy of these people blossoming like a rose in the last days. The native people of South America are most assuredly descendants of the family of Lehi, as are the native people of Central America, Mexico, the U.S., and Polynesia. This is without a doubt a people that is embracing the Book of Mormon and their heritage in the Gospel in great numbers today; that is no coincidence, but fulfillment of prophecy.

15. "Nevertheless, when that day cometh, saith the prophet, that they no more turn aside their hearts against the Holy One

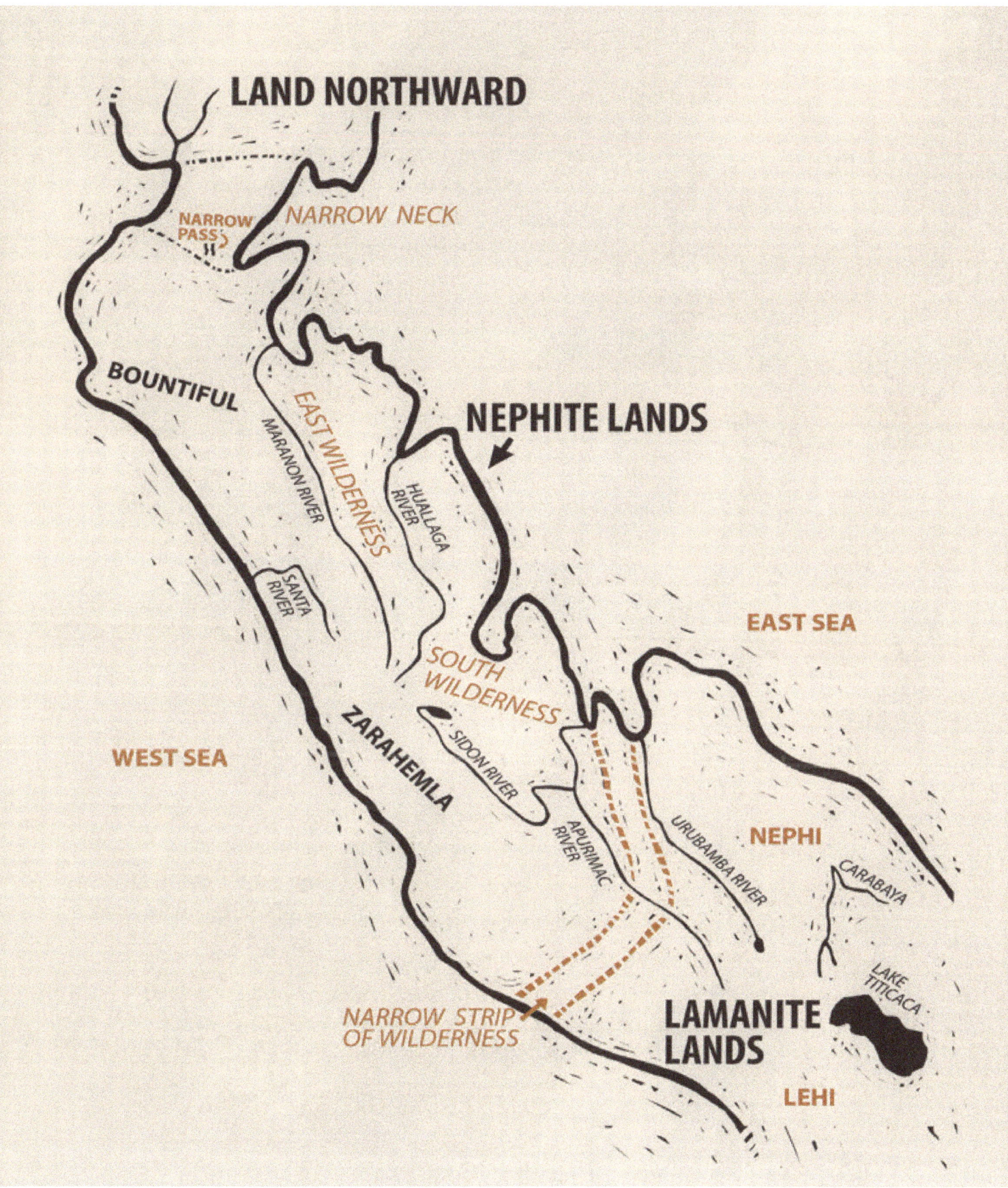

Figure #18 A more complete map of the geography of the Book of Mormon.

THE CITY OF NEPHI

of Israel, then will he remember the covenants which he made to their fathers.

16. Yea, then will he remember the isles of the sea; yea, and all the people who are of the house of Israel, will I gather in, saith the Lord, according to the words of the prophet Zenos, from the four quarters of the earth." 1Nephi 19:15-16

MODERN DAY GEOGRAPHY SUMMARY

Book of Mormon geography has been very illusive and difficult for many scholars over the years to sort out and to integrate the actual scriptures into the modern day scenario. What we do know that helps us clear the historical clouds of doubt are:

1. Lehi landed in Chile at the 30th parallel in South America.
2. Under certain conditions the ocean currents would have been favourable to land on the western coast of Chile.
3. The Land of South America as we know it today is considerably different than when Nephi built his city in 580 B.C., because the 'whole face of the land was changed.'
4. Nephi and Jacob say that they lived on an 'isle of the sea'.
5. The narrow neck of land with its narrow pass is a defining and important geographical clue to the Book of Mormon geography that needs to be properly identified.
6. The modern continent of South America today is considerably different today, but religious freedom has brought about the fulfillment of prophesies and promises that Nephi spoke of regarding these people who are a remnant of the House of Israel.

Chapter Note #1: This quote in the book *Jesus The Christ* references the same quote in Talmage's book, *The Articles of Faith* p. 259-260. This information in the *Articles of Faith* has been changed in more recent editions of the book presumably after the death of Elder Talmage to reflect the current trends of thought among the academics of our time, and is not the original version as first stated by Elder Talmage.

The original version of this statement can still be found in its first version in the book, *Jesus The Christ* p.55-56 chapter note #3.

Picture #17
The way the South American continent appears today with the Andean Mountain chain still clearly showing the land Southward, the Narrow Neck of Land, and the Land Northward.

THE CITY OF NEPHI

{Facing Picture Ch #6} The important ruins at Ollaytaytambo have a temple on top of the mountain that is completely terraced.

CHAPTER 6

BASIC THEORIES

There are a lot of theories regarding the Book of Mormon archaeology, geography, migrations, and peoples. So let's examine a few theories a little bit closer.

Archaeology of South America

The archaeology found in South America is quite diverse. A person can find literally the same types of pyramids, fortresses, and buildings that are found in the great Pre-Colombian cities of Mexico and Guatemala. There are many similarities in construction, design, actual dimensions, and age to these ancient ruins. The fact that many similarities in the archaeology exist in all the Americas is in fact quite significant. However, if one can look at Nephi as the great architect and founder of the Nephite nation, we will get a picture of the kind of archaeology of the Cusco area. Nephi was a builder of cities, a temple to God, and a righteous nation. Even though Nephi was starting from scratch in a new land, he would have left an undeniable legacy as a builder, as modest as it may have been to us, today. It is not hard to conceive of an area where Nephi built beautiful terraces, irrigation canals, aqueducts, and agricultural experiment stations. We can visualize a city which is protected by a huge walled fortress to protect against enemies. A temple containing four main rooms and the sun room would be more Nephi's style, than a huge pyramid that has no apparent usefulness other than as a high man-made mountain. The workmanship and 'manner of construction' would be more of a tell-tale sign of his life's work. Stone construction of 'Egyptian style' is what we are looking for in these ruins. Fountains, courtyards, and gardens that adorned the temple grounds were more likely the concepts of a prophet of God. There are no great ceremonial sacrificial altars used for human sacrifice in his thought process, only the wash basins and alters similar to the Temple of Solomon. The huge stepped platform type pyramids that would have taken thousands of people to build over hundreds of years would not have entered into Nephi's thinking nor would they have been useful to his people.

Archaeology of Mexico and Central America

In contrast to what we know about the Book of Mormon, much of the great civilizations and cities of the Aztecs (Mixtecs, Toltecs, and etc.) and Mayas do not fit the type of religious culture we envision from the pages of our scriptures. As one visits these impressive ruins, you cannot help but be impressed at the work and effort paid out centuries ago to build such colossal cities. And especially, what dictator or tyrant would heavily tax and subject his people to labor building such structures given the concept that we enjoy of our Heavenly Father and his gospel. Obviously, we know that many of these great civilizations built and grew up in centuries after the Nephite culture died out and the Lamanites went into apostasy. As much as these ruins all start to look the same, many are quite distinct and very interesting. An example is the Temple of Quetzalcoatl at Teotihuacan outside Mexico City; it has feathered fiery serpents which would be a good parallel to the Brazen Serpent lifted up to save the Children of Israel from snake bite in the desert which is mentioned in the Bible and also in the Book of Mormon. Can all of these civilizations be related somewhat or are they distinctive and separate? Are they all related because they come from a common source or a 'Mother' civilization? Was this center of civilization the Pre-Inca Empire that spread to the north countries as it expanded? What is the evidence that can suggest such migrations?

Migrations

The answer to some of these archaeological questions is in the Book of Mormon itself. In the year 55 B.C this sacred scripture talks about huge migrations that started to happen among the Nephites. These migrations always went to the north. We assume that they were able to build boats or get to Yucatan or Central America by raft, because these people were never heard of again.

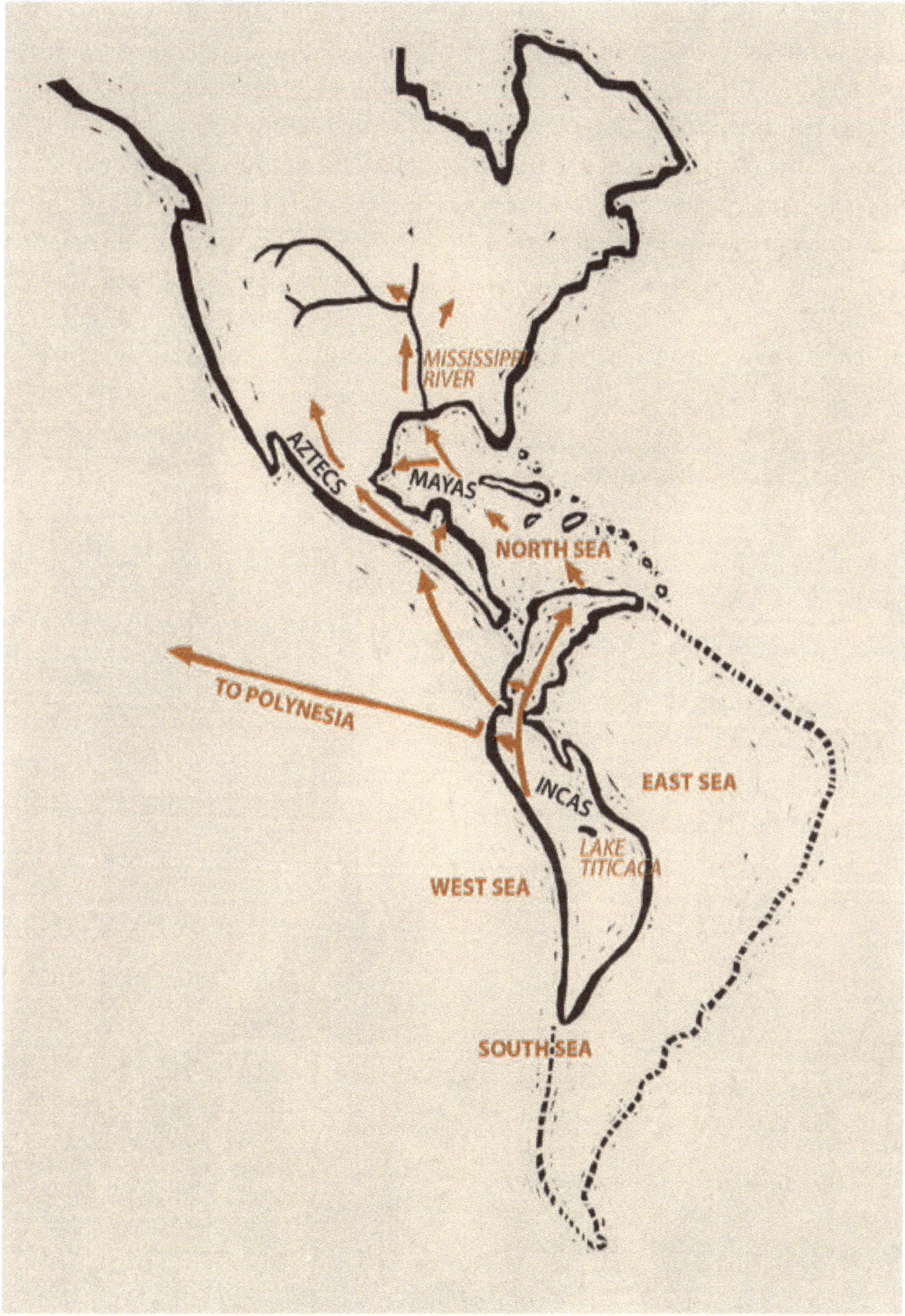

Figure #19 Map of the migrations of the people in the Book of Mormon.

Some of the migrations were very large; one group included 5400 men and their wives and children. Hagoth is said to have built a boat and took colonizers with him, they embarked at the narrow neck of land and traveled by boat northward. The first ship returned, and other boats were built and set sail again always to the North. It is important to note that

THE CITY OF NEPHI

these several groups that left were never heard of any more. This was at a time before the coming of Christ and before the land was changed. In our model of South America that would mean that Hagoth would have been free to launch his boat in the 'West Sea' (Pacific Ocean) and travel freely through the Darien Strait of Panama because that land mass didn't exist, and was under water. Such a waterway would allow them to travel to either side of Central America, either to the west coast, Pacific side, or the east coast, the Caribbean side of the continent. Such freedom would account for cities being built on both sides. Hagoth also could have launched his craft at the narrow neck of land which was common place and sailed west into Polynesia to establish civilizations in those lands as per the theory of Thor Heyerdahl and his book called the, *Kon Tiki*. The Book of Mormon relates this account in the following passage:

Picture #18 Migrations were generally to the north and usually accomplished by building boats or rafts. Some boats were extremely large and could carry many people.

9. And it came to pass that in this year there were many people who went forth into the land northward. And thus ended the thirty and eighth year." Alma 63:4-9

We only know about some of the migrations that are mentioned as a side note in the Book of Mormon. Mormon only mentions it because presumably the son of Alma, Corianton, went with one such migration, otherwise it may never have even made it into the sacred account. We do not know how many other groups became disenchanted and went looking for a new land. We also do not know how many other groups from the Jaredites and the Mulekites also had similar ambitions. These migrations were undoubtedly occurring since Jaredite times (2200 B.C.). They all arrived in the New World by boat, so it is not any stretch of the imagination to say that there could have been in all likelihood several groups who split from the 'Mother' civilization and struck out to find a better life.

All accounts we know about though were always to the **North** by boat or some other means. This would also seem to validate the theory that the main civilization in South America was where the foundation or center of their culture grew over the centuries, and then expanded to Polynesia and the Northern countries, especially Mexico, Yucatan Peninsula, Guatemala, and Central America.

Picture #19
Large reed boat built by native craftsmen on Lake Titicaca in Bolivia/Peru.

One question that might be asked is why do people leave an area and migrate to another region? As I have contemplated this question an answer comes from my own family history and the history of the Church. When a group of people are pursued and harassed and life made difficult by other peoples, then you do just as the early pioneers did who left their nice homes and abandoned their cities to migrate to a new land and start all over again. You have two options as a people: stay put in your lands and cities and be prepared to fight to protect yourself when your enemies come against you, or leave your lands and go somewhere new in search of peace and happiness. In the 1970's after three generations of farming and building up an area in Southern Nevada, my father took his family and all his possessions and migrated to a new land, Canada. Some of the reasons were government instability, poor economics for farming, over population, and an urge to do something different, to conquer a new land, and change our family's financial prospects for the future. We migrated not necessarily to get rich, but in search of a new life with better opportunities. Many of these Nephites in 70 B.C. found themselves in the same circumstances. Many were discontented and wanted something different and tired of being harassed and killed by the Lamanites, and hence the desire to migrate to new areas. Not many years later King Limhi moved his whole Nephite nation to Zarahemla from the Land of Nephi to escape the Lamanite aggression.

Why do we have such diversity in the Mayan, Aztec, and other cultures? It is interesting that there seems to be a time when all these groups in Mexico and Guatemala were isolated and developed there own distinct cultures from each other. Even though mainly things are the same there are striking differences as well in the cultures. It could be that after the land changed, and the coming of Christ to the Americas, that access to some of these areas was cut off, hence the isolation. This would be a good case for the Mayan and the Yucatan Peninsula peoples. Also, during a period of prosperity and righteousness, such as after the coming of Christ to the Americas, the desire to leave and go somewhere else was nonexistent. People simply were happy and stayed put in their cities for the next two hundred plus years.

Polynesian Peoples

As a young man I remember being intrigued by the writings of Thor Heyerdahl and his book, *Kon Tiki*. His theory was that because the Polynesians believe that they originate from a 'land of the reeds' that these people migrated from Peru/Bolivia centuries ago. To prove his theory he set out to go to the Lake Titicaca region in Bolivia, 'land of the reeds' and have the native Bolivians build him a boat using all local materials that could navigate the ocean currents. After he had his reed boat made and equipped with balsa wood for masts, he transported his boat to the west coast of Ecuador. He laid in provisions and earthen jars for water, etc. and launched forth his craft into the ocean not far from where Hagath would have launched his boat. The currents that time of year took him steadily west and eventually to the Easter Islands. Ref 13 Thor Heyerdahl.

Theory on Polynesian Origins

A short excerpt summary from Thor Heyerdahl's writings is included here because of his belief that the origins of the Polynesians actually came from Peru. He learned of the legends that the tall bearded white or fair-skinned people were all killed in a civil war is exactly what we have in scripture from the Book of Mormon. Heyerdahl claims that the Cari Indians (Pre-Incan natives) came from the Coquimbo Valley in Northern Chile (Site of the first Lehi Landing). The presentation is as follows:

"Heyerdahl claimed that in Incan legend there was a sun-god named Con-Tici Viracocha who was the supreme head of the mythical fair-skinned people in Peru. The original name for Viracocha was *Kon-Tiki* or *Illa-Tiki*, which means *Sun-Tiki* or *Fire-Tiki*. Kon-Tiki was high priest and sun-king of these legendary 'white men' who left enormous ruins on the shores of Lake Titicaca. The legend continues with the mysterious bearded white men being attacked by a chief named Cari who came from the Coquimbo Valley. They had a battle on an island in Lake Titicaca, and the fair race was massacred. However, Kon-Tiki and his closest companions managed to escape and later arrived on the Pacific coast. The legend ends with Kon-Tiki and his companions disappearing westward out to sea.

When the Spaniards came to Peru, Heyerdahl asserted, the Incas told them that the colossal monuments that stood deserted about the landscape were erected by a race of white gods who had lived there before the Incas themselves became rulers. The Incas described these 'white gods' as wise, peaceful instructors who had originally come from the north in the 'morning of time' and taught the Incas' primitive forebears architecture as well as manners and customs. They were unlike other Native Americans in that they had 'white skins and long beards' and were taller than the Incas. The Incas said that the 'white gods' had then left as suddenly as they had come and fled westward across the Pacific. After they had left, the Incas themselves took over power in the country.

Heyerdahl said that when the Europeans first came to the Pacific islands, they were astonished that they found some of the natives to have relatively light skins and beards. There were whole families that had pale skin, hair varying in color from reddish to blonde. In contrast, most of the Polynesians had golden-brown skin, raven-black hair, and rather flat noses. Heyerdahl claimed that when Jakob Roggeveen first discovered Easter Island in 1722, he supposedly noticed that many of the natives were white-skinned. Heyerdahl claimed that these people could count their ancestors who were 'white-skinned' right back to the time of Tiki and Hotu Matua, when they first came sailing across the sea 'from a mountainous land in the east which was scorched by the sun.' The ethnographic evidence for these claims is outlined in Heyerdahl's book *Aku Aku: The Secret of Easter Island*.

Heyerdahl proposed that Tiki's neolithic people colonized the then-uninhabited Polynesian islands as far north as Hawaii, as far south as New Zealand, as far east as Easter Island, and as far west as Samoa and Tonga around 500 AD. They supposedly sailed from Peru to the Polynesian islands on *pae-paes*—large rafts built from balsa logs, complete with sails and each with a small cottage. They built enormous stone statues carved in the image of human beings on Pitcairn, the Marquesas, and Easter Island that resembled those in Peru. They also built huge pyramids on Tahiti and Samoa with steps like those in Peru. But all over Polynesia, Heyerdahl found indications that Tiki's peaceable race had not been able to hold the islands alone for long. He found evidence that suggested that seagoing war canoes as large as Viking ships and lashed together two and two had brought Stone Age Northwest American Indians to Polynesia around 1100AD, and they mingled with Tiki's people. The oral history of the people of Easter Island, at least as it was documented by Heyerdahl, is completely consistent with this theory, as is the archaeological record he examined (Heyerdahl 1958). In particular, Heyerdahl obtained a radiocarbon date of 400 AD for a charcoal fire located in the pit that was held by the people of Easter Island to have been used as an 'oven' by the 'Long Ears,' which Heyerdahl's Rapa Nui sources, reciting oral tradition, identified as a white race which had ruled the island in the past." (Ref. 26 - Heyerdahl 1957)

The Polynesian people in deed are of the House of Israel and a chosen people in the Last Days that have originated from the 'Mother Civilization' of the Book of Mormon.

Picture #20
Large reed boats can last for many years before they become water-logged and non-serviceable. They are very stable and can endure severe storms and waves.

In the book, *Lehi, Father of Polynesia*, Bruce S. Sutton, (Ref# 23) publishes a genealogical chart that establishes the Polynesian ancestry from Tiki in 387A.D. all the way back to Manco Capac or Nephi (the 1st Inca King) and from there to Lehi and through the Book of Mormon genealogy of Manasseh back to Adam. It is without a doubt that the Maori/Hawaiian traditions and legends lend credence to the fact that not only did **Christ visit the islands of Polynesia but also that they also came from the 'Mother Civilization' of the Nephites, from the 'land of the reeds'.** Chapter Notes #1

Geography of the Book of Mormon

Theories of the Geography of the Book of Mormon are numerous. Many people believe that the Book of Mormon geography pertains to the Mayans in Guatemala and the Yucatan, or of the great civilizations of Mexico, or of the many ancient sites that are found in the U.S. There can be good cases made for any of these areas. However, one of the most underrated and overlooked region is that of Peru and South America.

Figure #20 Modern topographical map showing the elevations of the Andean Mountains.

120 BASIC THEORIES

Why is that? Probably the reason is because of the way the land changed and the image we get of what the land should look like after reading and studying the Book of Mormon. The shape of South America's land mass just does not initially strike one as the place where the history of the Book of Mormon took place. But as a person studies the possibilities and the clues in the Book of Mormon the more it becomes clear that it is not only a plausible explanation but also a good workable theory. The geography theory of this book is based on the place of Lehi's landing, the location of the narrow neck of land, and the total logistical dimensions that would have to be satisfied.

Nephi was a great prophet and a very intelligent and skilful writer. He did not include many geographic details in his account on purpose so that he would have more room for the precious things of life and what would ultimately be of greatest benefit to us and his descendants. There are still many clues from the Book of Mormon that help us to identify and affix the geography elements to the Andean Highlands. The narrow neck of land in the Gulf of Guayaquil, the landing position of Lehi's family, the actual trek of 'many days' approximately 1000 miles into the wilderness by Nephi to establish his city in Cusco, Peru, are all evidences that point to this area as the geographical area in which the Book of Mormon took place.

Two Hill Cumorah Theory

There will always be lots of different theories until more revelation or light is given us either when the Lord comes again or when a prophet actually speaks on this subject. Then knowledge will replace our theories. However, until then, one theory that is important to explore would be the 'Two Hill Cumorah theory'. What is suggested in this phrase is that there were actually two Hill Cumorahs. This Hill Cumorah or Hill Ramah for the Jaredite culture was identified in the Book of Mormon.

> 6 "And it came to pass that when we had gathered in all our people in one to the land of Cumorah, behold I, Mormon, began to be old; and knowing it to be the last struggle of my people, and having been commanded of the Lord that I should not suffer the records which had been handed down by our fathers, which were sacred, to fall into the hands of the Lamanites, (for the Lamanites would destroy them) therefore I made this record out of the plates of Nephi, and hid up in the **hill Cumorah** all the records which had been entrusted to me by the hand of the Lord, save it were these few plates which I gave unto my son Moroni." Mormon 6:6

This hill was where the Prophet Mormon led the Nephites in the last great battle when the Nephites were defeated and ultimately exterminated. When Limhi's people originally found the area they had wandered for again '***many days***' (170-200 days) and were lost. As was shown before this area to the North could have really only been several hundred miles at most. Spatially speaking, New York State and the modern Hill Cumorah is nearly 6000 miles away from the proposed site in Venezuela. Just as in the preface to this book, it is ridiculous to think that Mormon's Hill Cumorah and the Jaredites Hill Ramah could be the same hill in the State of New York because of the distances involved even if there was a land bridge between the two continents.

Joseph Smith actually never was known to call the modern hill in the State of New York by the name of the Hill Cumorah during his lifetime. The name of the Hill Cumorah was applied to it subsequently. So, how did Moroni get the plates to upstate New York in Joseph Smith's day? Moroni was a resurrected being, a glorified being of flesh and bone. He had the plates in his hands when he showed them to Joseph and the other witnesses. He came and got them from Joseph when the Lord took away his translating privileges for a season. It is not hard to imagine Moroni transporting the plates in his resurrected form, to the modern hill along with the Urim and Thumin, and placing them in a stone box he fashioned for the purpose of storing the plates until the arrival of Joseph Smith. There is no doubt until we get more divine information, that what we know is that there was only one ancient Hill Cumorah where the Nephites were annihilated. Whether or not the modern Hill Cumorah is the place of the great last battle does not matter, it was factually the place where Joseph Smith recovered the plates and started us on this great journey in the Last Days. This book suggests though that they were two separate places many miles apart (6000), one in South America and the other in upper state, New York. Therefore, the theory of two 'Hill Cumorahs' helps us to understand how all of things can properly relate to each other many centuries apart.

Christ in the Americas

Why do ancient traditions and legends in Polynesia and Central America have Christ coming to their lands and teaching their peoples? Given the previous discussion it becomes apparent that the culture of the Pre-Inca/Andean motherland of the Nephite civilization was exported to these other areas. More and more archaeological evidence is being discovered all the time that suggests growing similarities in their cultures. It is not a large leap then that these traditions would migrate with the people before and after the time of Christ. There is also the obvious possibility that Christ could have gone to each of these peoples and taught them individually in their own lands.

21. "And verily I say unto you, that ye are they of whom I said: Other sheep I have which are not of his fold; them also I must bring, and they shall hear my voice; and there shall be one fold, and one Shepard.

1. And verily, verily, I say unto you that I have **other sheep, which are not of this land, neither of the land of Jerusalem, neither in any parts of that land round about** whither I have been to minister.

2. For they of whom I speak are they who have not as yet heard my voice; neither have I at any time manifested myself unto them.

3. But I have received a commandment of the Father that I shall go unto them, and that they shall hear my voice, and shall be numbered among my sheep, that there may be one fold and one shepherd; therefore I go to show myself unto them." 3Nephi 15:21 & 3Nephi 16:1-3

Jesus Christ does mention that he has 'Other Sheep' that he must bring. This scripture tells us that Jesus Christ had other peoples that he had to visit and teach other than the Jews in Jerusalem and the Nephites and Lamanites who were in the Land Bountiful. This reference could be made about the 'Lost Ten Tribes' or it could also actually refer to the other Nephite/Lamanite peoples who migrated north to Central and North America or west to Polynesia to their new lands. After the time of Christ, the land changed, and there was not the previous water route to the Yucatan and other areas as in previous times. This would have isolated the Mayan and other cultures to develop on their own and actually necessitated a visit from Jesus Christ so that they could be taught and receive the Gospel. The Polynesian peoples of Hawaii and other places also have compelling traditions or legends of Christ's visit to them in their lands.

BUILDING OF PYRAMIDS

The building of Pyramids in the Archaeology of the Pre-Columbian Native Americans is a very amazing phenomenon. There are pyramids in various places such as Peru, Yucatan, Guatemala, and Mexico. Many are similar in construction and some are quite different. The Temple of the Sun and the Temple of the Moon at Teotihuacán and the pyramid of Cholula just out side of Mexico City are the largest pyramids in the world which includes the pyramids of Egypt. The fact that there are pyramids in all these civilizations points to the theory that they could have common origin. The Mulekites and Lehi's party all migrated from Jerusalem to South America and had knowledge of Egyptian civilization, and as these groups migrated north from the 'Mother Civilization' of course they took these concepts with them into their new lands.

The Olmec Culture pertains to the time period of the Jaredites (2200 B.C.) and has their origin in Northern Ecuador and Venezuela and also central Mexico. They were known to have built pyramids both in South America and Mexico. Erin Cridlin in his paper, <u>The Native Olmec Indians</u> in PageWise writes the following about the Olmec Culture:

> "After further investigation and archaeological research on the Olmec, it was learned for certain that they were the mother culture of South America. The Olmec calendar, writing and some of the Olmec gods are present in more evolved forms in descending cultures. Some archaeologists believe that Quetzalcoatl, the plumed serpent god of the Aztec and Maya, originated with the Olmec. The jaguar is believed to have been the principle god of the Olmec and appears as the god of rain in later cultures. Unlike the later South American civilizations, the Olmec portrayed very few animals as deities, only the jaguar, monkey, eagle, falcon and serpent.
>
> The Olmec Indians were the first to build the stone pyramids in South America. The pyramids were made from basalt and the first was built near modern day La Venta, Mexico around 900 BC. The pyramids of the Olmec were very similar to the pyramids built by later cultures, very tall and narrow with steep staircases on each of the four sides leading up to a platform at the top where ceremonial rituals, including blood-letting and human sacrifice were performed.

The Olmec inhabited areas ranging from rural lands to small towns to large cities. The largest cities contained thousands of people. Olmec society was divided into classes by wealth and social status. The ruling class lived in the large cities and towns while the lower class resided in less populated areas. The Olmec rulers were also priests and possessed both religious and political power. The lower class farmed and hunted for a living, while the upper class mainly traded art and other luxury items.

Around 500 BC, the Olmec culture began to decline, although archaeologists are not sure why. Some attribute the collapse of the civilization to depleted resources and others say social distress between the classes. Whatever the cause, the Olmec collapsed and the people went on to different places and formed new civilizations, but they kept the Olmec traditions and beliefs." Ref 16

We certainly know the reason why the Olmec (Jaredite) Culture declined was because of the civil wars which completely devastated an entire civilization. There are many pyramids in South America which would indicate a connection between them and the cultures in Egypt, Mexico and other areas where these man-made structures occur. The following discussion and pictures are an example of pyramids in South America done by J.M. Allen:

"But when we turn to South America, the pyramids get bigger, bolder, and older.

At Cochasqui in Ecuador there is a little known pyramid complex linked to astronomical alignments.

Tiahuanaco until recently considered the oldest city in the Americas has the largely un-excavated Akapana pyramid with internal water channels, sometimes said to be a site for refining tin.

The city of Chan Chan on the Peruvian coast had a giant adobe pyramid which the Spanish engineers diverted a river to so they could wash its bulk away in their search for some hidden treasure.

The North of Peru is rich of interesting places like Trujillo, Chiclayo and the lost world of the Chachapoyas. The Pre-Columbian Chachapoyas culture, conquered in the 15th century by the Incas, has left a landscape scattered with villages and burial sites which until recently has been largely overlooked by archaeologists. Situated in the cloud forests around the town of Chachapoyas in Peru's northern Amazonas Department, these sites are dominated by the mighty fortress of Kuelap, perched majestically atop mountain-top cliffs overlooking the verdant Andean landscape. In Chachapoyas, remnants of the past invite discovery by the bold adventurer, and the cultures of the present extend a friendly welcome. In Chiclayo lies the tomb of the Lord of Sipan (the richest tomb discovered in the Americas), the Valley of the 26 pyramids of Tucume and Bruning Museum where there is an interesting collection of gold artefacts and ceramics The pyramids of the Sun and Moon, just south of Trujillo, are the largest structures ever put up in South America, and are second in the Western Hemisphere only to the Pyramid of Cholula, Mexico, in size. They formed the spiritual center of the Moche Empire, a highly sophisticated yet mysterious culture that pre-dated the Incas by nearly 1000 years. It is quite certain that the Moche Indians had contact with other civilizations in the ancient Americas, and there is good reason to believe they may have been influenced by Asian ocean- going voyagers as well. The Pyramid of the Moon contains a central, vaulted chamber, and the mountain directly behind, Cerro Blanco, appears to have been shaped by humans into a pyramid form as well. Huanchaco is a fishing town where "caballitos de totoro" are still used by the local inhabitants, who venture into the cold currents of the Pacific in these precarious-looking reed boats. This massive adobe city, really a series of royal compounds built by the Chimu, was a major source of gold for both the Incas, and later, for the Spanish. Though well-looted over the centuries, gold artefacts still occasionally appear in the drifting sands. Contacts between Chan Chan and the Asian continent have never been proven, but there are tantalizing hints. Pottery figures depict Asiatic men with beards and turbans; even the name 'Chan Chan' seems to be Chinese in origin.

At Tucume, again in Peru, Thor Heyerdahl found the pyramids to be so massive that at first they were thought to be natural mountains. The largest of these measuring some 1,476 x 328 x 131ft is rectangular in shape with its longest side almost double that of the Great Pyramid in Egypt.

At Trujillo in Peru, the Pyramids of the Sun and the Moon date from the Moche period of around 600AD and used 140 million adobe bricks in their construction.

And the latest site discovered, again in Peru in the Supe valley is at Caral where the pyramids are said to date to 2627BC - making them older than the first Egyptian pyramids.

At the well known site of Machu Picchu - said to be the last stronghold of the Inca and built on a sheer mountain top, the casual visitor is probably unaware that the valley below along the edge of the Vilcobamba River contains a giant flat topped pyramid, engineered so that it is only visible at certain times of the year. This kind of sacred engineering seems to have been a feature of ancient American cultures.

On the Marcahuasi plateau in Peru, there exist numerous giant sculptures including a Sphinx-like head, but these features can only be seen properly from a key vantage point.
In Bolivia, not far from the petrified or enchanted city of Pumiri, is to be seen a 'Cheops'-like pyramid in the distance, but closer inspection at any other angle suggests it is a natural mountain. Similarly at a remote site in the village of St Bartolome on the Bolivian Altiplano, a part of a pyramid is seen to be propped up against a natural rock face.

In ancient South America it would seem, natural features sometimes look man-made and man-made features look natural, why build a whole pyramid when from where you are standing the landscape can be improved by building or improving a site to give the *appearance* of a pyramid in the distance!

Reaching across the Atlantic to the Canary Islands, step pyramids are also to be found on the island of Tenerife where the complex known as the Pyramids of Guimar have been investigated by Thor Heyerdahl. Did ancient explorers from the Americas stop this way on their way to the Mediterranean? These are flat-topped pyramids in the American style since the majority of American pyramids were flat-topped stepped platforms often with a small temple on the top, not unlike the ziggurats of Mesopotamia, but Egyptian pyramids, with the exception of the stepped pyramid at Saqarra which is one of the earliest ones, were largely smooth faced and sharply pointed." Ref 17 J.M.Allen 14th November 2002

Figure #21 Pyramid of Pacaritanpu is uniquely designed to capture the sun's rays at different times of the year. At the solstice the windows of the pyramid light up. The pyramid is part of the larger 'Tree of Life' in the Sacred Valley.

Pyramids are probably the most famous and visible remains or ruins of these indigenous people, however, we must be aware that even though Nephi and his people no doubt had knowledge of Egyptian pyramids they most likely never built any of them in their lifetime. The thousands of people necessary to build such structures, the desire and inclination to build them, and the hundreds of years of peace time to accomplish such colossal building projects were not inspired by Nephi and the early Nephite prophets and leaders. Their desires and efforts were directed more toward building their homes, protecting themselves, building canals and terraces for farming, and a temple to worship their God. There could be one exception to this theory, the Pyramid of Pacaritanpu.

Pyramid of Pacaritanpu

There is a very special pyramid in the Sacred Valley of the Incas called the Pyramid of Pacaritanpu. Its origin is very old and probably dates to the Chavin Culture period of time, some 500-550 B.C. This great pyramid is very large in land size encompassing many hectares in area. Nevertheless, it is not very tall in height and was built on the valley floor. It is different from most other Pre-Inca ruins in that it was not built on the side or top of a mountain. The ancient builders were more concerned about its design and function than its altitude. It is simply a system of terraces built into the agricultural landscape and part of the larger design of the 'Tree of Life' talked about earlier.

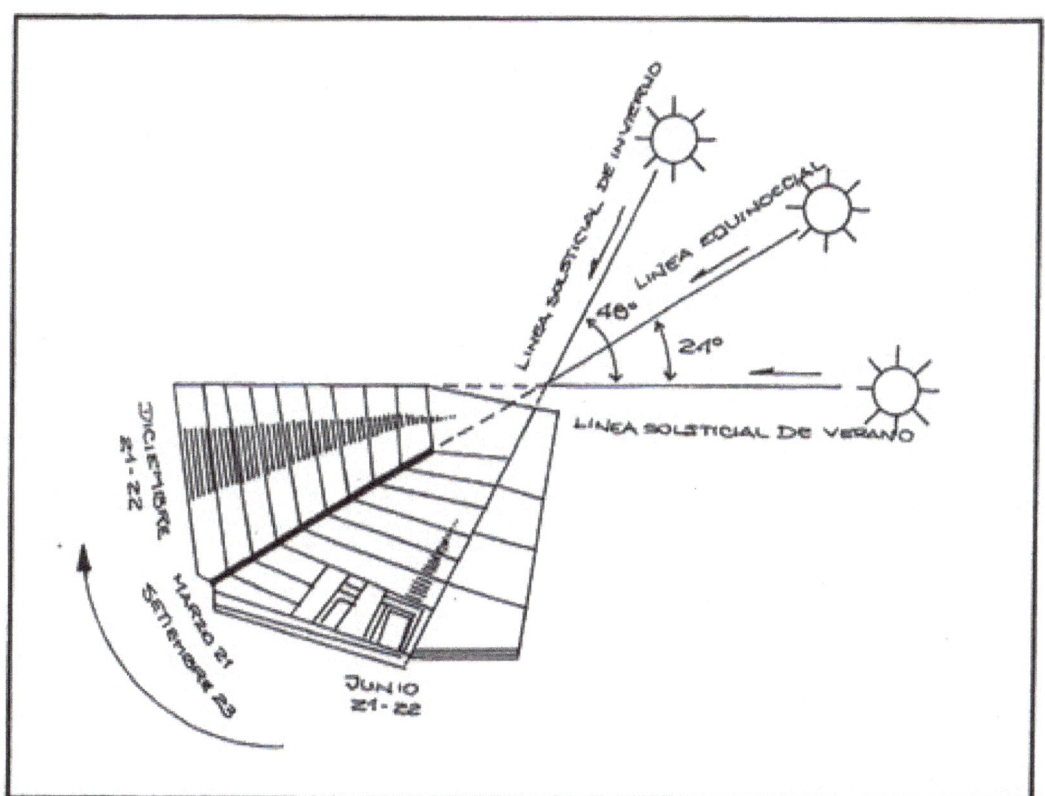

Figure #22 This diagram of the Pyramid of Pacaritanpu shows the direction of the sun at various times during the year. Very precise engineering was employed to build the pyramid to function as a sundial for the Chavin people.

Picture #21 At first glance the Pyramid of Pacaritanpu does not look like anything at all especially an ancient pyramid, only neatly organized farming terraces. Upon close study and observation it becomes a marvel of Peru.

  The Pyramid of Pacaritanpu or 'House of the Dawn' as the natives refer to it is truly one of the most remarkable ruins in all of the Pre-Inca sites in Peru. The thought and engineering that went into its construction make it stand out as a significant feat even though the manpower and effort to create this structure was not on the same scale as other colossal pyramids.

THE CITY OF NEPHI

Picture #22 The Ruins of Tambomachay are called the 'Resting Place'.

The Ruins of Tambomachay

There is a legend or theory from the Ruins of Tambomachay that makes it a remarkable place to include in our study. The site was a ceremonial bathing place called the 'resting place'. Actually the source of the spring water that flows into the fountains are still unknown even today. The ruins do exist close to our Book of Mormon city or Land of Shemlon which was the city of the Lamanite guardians during the time of King Noah. The theory is that the priests of the wicked King Noah stole the twenty-four Lamanite princesses while they were bathing or at the resting place making themselves merry.

Machu Picchu

The wicked priests of Noah, who were the followers of the priest, Amulon, stole the daughters of the Lamanites and took them away to the remote city of Machu Pichu. This most famous ancient Peruvian ruin has a legend associated with it being called the city of the 'Chosen Women'. An adventurer and explorer, Yale professor, Hiram Bingham found the ancient ruins of Machu Picchu in 1911. Hiram Bingham in his book, *Lost City of the Incas,* says that the vast majority of human remains found at Machu Picchu were female. This caused Hiram Bingham and the other researchers to identify the city as a convent or a place for 'Chosen Women'. Could the remote beautiful city actually be the place where the priests of King Noah fled with their captive Lamanite brides? It is approximately thirty miles away from Cusco in a beautiful remote area which would have been an ideal hideout for Amulon and his men. Bingham found more than fifty female and only four male human remains.

Picture #23
The famous Peruvian ruins of Machu Pichu

132 BASIC THEORI

BUILDING OF TEMPLES

    The building of Temples is a unique characteristic of a chosen and covenant people. If we take a quick look at known historical accounts of the Lord's covenant people we get a certain pattern that is very consistent. We know starting with Adam that he built an altar to God. Abraham made his altar on a threshing floor on top of Mount Moriah. Moses was instructed on his Mount Sinai and his Tabernacle in the wilderness. King Solomon built God a magnificent temple with a paid work force of over 200,000 men working seven years to complete it. The covenant people of Israel kept rebuilding the temple through the centuries after wars and destruction down to its final destruction by the Roman Empire in 70 A.D. The Temple of Solomon was the 'Navel of the World, the Center of the Universe' in Jerusalem and for the Israelite nation for many centuries. Joseph Smith's first mandate when the saints gathered to Zion in Kirtland was to build a temple. As the Latter-Day covenant people gathered to Independence and Far West, temples were planned and corner stones were laid. Then finally, came the red brick store and the beautiful Nauvoo Temple. All these structures were built with meager means monetarily and with little manpower. They were truly a sacrifice to the early saints. After the exodus to the west and the Salt Lake valley, again the covenant people were called upon to build temples. Temples in St. George, Manti, Logan and the Endowment House in Salt Lake City were built under adverse pioneer conditions in the frontier and from the poverty of the saints. The Salt Lake temple was planned and started on the first day that Brigham Young surveyed his new land, but it took 40 years to complete. Later chapters of this book are devoted to the temple that Nephi built after the 'manner of construction of the Temple of Solomon' and what that means exactly.

    There is a pattern to the temple building of the Lord's covenant people. He has always required His People to build temples to worship Him and receive His instruction. Many times it is a simple altar on a mountain top, but always it is a functional place where covenants can be made, revelation and instruction given, and ordinances performed. If the covenant people are capable and prosperous more is expected and sacrifice is always required. Temples throughout history have always been sacred, beautiful, functional facilities for the specific purposes of the Lord. They have never been the lavish palaces of King Solomon (which later took him 14 years to build), or the high towers of Babel to get to Heaven. Similarly, the large pyramids and lavish palaces which generally constitute the modern day ruins of South America, Mexico, and Egypt do not fit the pattern of temple

Picture #24
The uniquely carved walls and stone work of the Temple of Koricancha.

building and worship that the Lord has instituted among his people. These structures were built on the backs of the oppressed by wicked monarchs for no apparent reason or function except to gratify their pride and self-aggrandizement. These wicked and perverse generations of men have been inspired and sponsored by Satan himself. He has been attempting to lead the Children of Men astray from the very beginning of time. It is interesting that many of the cultures and places where you see pyramids today are places that once had the Gospel Light and then apostatized and turned to paganism because of wicked powerful men. Egypt is a good example of an area where Joseph introduced a covenant people and righteousness and then subsequently wicked rulers seized power and forced the people to build these colossal pyramids and cities.

So, in summary the Archeological ruins of the Andean Highlands lends itself well to the conceived Nephite culture and civilization, there are no huge pyramids in Cusco or the surrounding area. The obvious exception to this rule is the Pyramid of Pacaritanpu. Obviously, later building projects that are quite impressive today were built by apostates and remnants of this once great chosen people after their civilization was destroyed. Migrations

Picture #25
Reed Islands on Lake Titicaca, 'Land of the Reeds' were where the people lived with expertise for building reed boats that could be used for ocean-going vessels.

occurred that resulted in a dissemination of this culture to the north into areas of Central America, the Yucatan, and Mexico. The Polynesians have also had their roots traced back to this 'Mother Civilization' or 'Land of the Reeds'. Traditions have even linked their genealogies back to Manco Capac, or Nephi, the founder of the great civilization of Cusco, Peru.

Theories of the geography, the two hill Cumorahs, Christ visiting the Americas, and the building of pyramids were all discussed with our particular interest in their relationship to the Book of Mormon. The building of temples is a far different enterprise for a covenant people than the building of pyramids and other facilities that are inspired in the hearts of wicked men.

Chapter Notes:
1. The Bolivia/Peru area of Lake Titicaca is often called the 'land of the reeds' because historically as far back as tradition and legend can be traced, the people who lived around this high altitude lake made their homes and boats out of the reeds that grow profusely surrounding the crystal blue waters. The reeds were also made into floating platforms that people used to build their homes out on top of the lake for defensive purposes. The fame of these native reed boat builders caused Thor Heyerdahl to enlist their help in constructing his modern ocean-going reed boat in *Kon Tiki*.

{Facing Picture Ch #7} The great fortress of Sacsahuaman that protected the Inca capitol city, Cusco in ancient and colonial times.

CHAPTER 7

CHARACTERISTICS OF THE CITY OF NEPHI

A New Society

The City of Nephi was the home of the great prophet Nephi. It was where he lived for more than 45 years according to his brother Jacob, and it was where he died and was buried. This city that he loved and built not only carried his name but would have been an extension of the traits and qualities of the man we know as the Prophet Nephi. So, we want to reconstruct this ancient city by looking at the verses in the Book of Mormon that tell us about Nephi and what was important to him. Also, later when King Zeniff and his son King Noah, and grandson King Limhi reinhabit the city and rebuilt it to fit their needs, we get some important characteristics of the beautiful City of Nephi. Here is Nephi's first description of his new land and civilization:

> "And we did observe to keep the judgments, and the statutes, and the commandments of the Lord in all things, according to the Law of Moses.

> 11. And the Lord was with us; and we did prosper exceedingly; for we did sow seed, and we did reap again in abundance. And we began to raise flocks, and herds, and animals of every kind." 2Nephi 5:10-11

Nephi and his brethren were ambitious and hard working. They pitched their tents in their new city and then they started to build buildings, plant their crops, and tend their herds. We do not need to suppose that they would have immediately had a huge beautiful city overnight. This city took Nephi's lifetime and in fact many generations to reach its climax or apex, and four and one half centuries to finally become the great City of Nephi. However, having a prophet of God in charge means that the overall design or layout of the city would have probably come at the beginning under Nephi's direction.

> "And I did teach my people to build buildings, and to work in all manner of wood, and of iron, and of copper, and of brass, and of steel, and of gold, and of silver, and of precious ores, which were in great abundance.
> And I, Nephi, did build a temple; and I did construct it after the manner of the temple of Solomon save it were not built of so many precious things; for they were not to be found upon the land, wherefore, it could not be built like unto Solomon's temple. But the manner of the construction was like unto the temple of Solomon; and the workmanship thereof was exceedingly fine.
> And it came to pass that I, Nephi, did cause my people to be industrious, and to labor with their hands." 2Nephi 5:15-17

City Protection

One of the first concerns for Nephi was how to protect his people from the Lamanites that would eventually be attacking their city and possessions. So, Nephi, first made swords for their protection modeled after the Sword of Laban.

> "And I, Nephi, did take the sword of Laban, and after the manner of it did make many swords, lest by any means the people who were now called Lamanites should come upon us and destroy us; for I knew their hatred towards me and my children and those who were called my people." 2Nephi 5:14

Because of this concern it is not hard to imagine that Nephi would have had a good plan of defence for the city to protect his people when attacked. We would be assured that he would devise a fortress or walls or refuges from which to fight the Lamanites. Later, we find out that during the time of King Limhi the city had towers, walls, secret passage ways, and places of resort, all built with the defence of the city in mind.

Nephi as a City Planner

We know that many modern prophets have had the opportunity to plan cities and create them using a grid pattern with the temple as the center focal point. The city radiates out from the temple in all four directions. This seems to be a revealed pattern for city construction that the Lord considers to be the best for his covenant people. It would therefore be the possible pattern that Nephi also employed. The Temple of Nephi would be in the center with the four main roads or highways radiating out from the cardinal points of the compass, creating four quadrants of the city. If the construction was like the Temple of Solomon then the temple and the city would also be in the northern part of the top of the valley or mount. Nephi would have to plan the city's infrastructure of water canals, roads, city walls, towers, housing, and civic buildings to meet their current and future needs. As the prophet and king he most likely would have been given divine inspiration regarding all of these important functions of the city which would eventually become the model capitol city for the empire and the 'Center of the Universe, the Navel of the World' in the 'Land of Promise'. It was the beautiful capitol city of the Nephite Culture for about four hundred and fifty years.

The City at Nephi's Time

Let us imagine the different attributes of this city at the time of Nephi during his lifetime. First of all there would be many well built buildings and that the people of Nephi would be proud of their workmanship. Of course the main featured building would be the temple which we will discuss at length in a later chapter. The city would need to be protected by a fortress or have a refuge to go to in the event of an attack. Any good leader would have as a major priority the defence of his city and so the time and energy to build these facilities would be important. Nephi would have wanted to explore the whole entire region and set up outposts to give advance warning to the people of the approach of an enemy in each direction. We can imagine that in the beginning the city was small and

Figure #23 Cusco city plan showing the Temple of Koricancha in the center.

modest, because the needs and the work force were modest, but we should not underestimate Nephi and his people. They were industrious and did work with their hands, and by all accounts were ambitious and excited about their new land.

Nephi would want to know where the different mineral deposits would be. He would be interested in metallurgical minerals such as gold for the manufacture of plates to be used for the writing of the Book of Mormon thirty years after they left Jerusalem. Minerals to make metal that could be forged into farm and cooking implements and weapons for defence. He would be very interested in rock quarries, in fountains, and water courses that could be diverted for drinking water and to irrigation canals for crop irrigation. Nephi would also be interested in the seasons, when to plant, when the rains would come, when the dry periods were. All these things would be critical to the leader of a new nation. For a group of people wandering for many days through a vast landscape of virgin territory and vistas of unpopulated wilderness, Nephi would have his choice of any land he wanted. And with the Liahona and guidance from the Lord, Nephi most likely found the choicest of all places in the 'Promised Land', and a land that was the choicest of all the lands in the Americas. It would be a land that was '**Choice Above All Other Lands**', and the Lord's choice that He had saved and prepared for them.

The City of Nephi would undoubtedly be situated in a very large beautiful mountain valley where the climate was cool and pleasurable, not hot and arid like the coast. It would be a beautiful area with very fertile soil, and running rivers or streams to provide fresh water for drinking, cleaning, and crops. Nephi would have been very interested in agriculture and feeding and clothing his people. There would have been provisions for agricultural experiment stations to develop new crop varieties and animal breeds and how they responded to different elevations or altitudes in the mountain valleys. Nephi would lay out the streets and buildings after a manner that he had seen before in Jerusalem or in Egypt. Starting a civilization from scratch he could plan and do whatever he wanted in this virgin land. Also, if the Lord instructed him on such things as building a boat or making tools, surely the Lord would also inspire and reveal to Nephi how to build this great city which would be the home of the Nephites from approximately 590-580 B.C. to 130 B.C. or about 450 years in total. Then later, it would be inhabited again by the Nephites by King Zeniff for another three generations. We also know that the city was inhabited by the Lamanites as their chief city and at different times and maybe even the Nephites again during the 200 plus years of peace after the visit of Jesus Christ. We have no

Picture #26 The native Peruvians are still known today to be an industrious people with talent for agriculture, textiles, pottery, and metallurgy.

record of the destruction of this great city at the coming of Christ. It is not on any of the lists of cities destroyed or rebuilt, so we presume that such a great city would have been mentioned if it had been destroyed. Therefore, we assume that it survived the destructions and that there should be evidence of this great stone-built city today.

Surrounding Valleys and Areas

Over time with exploration and expansion of the Nephite culture it would become very important for Nephi to also command the surrounding areas. Sending out people to colonize and develop different areas would be a natural extension to this new civilization. Surrounding valleys would be important both for development of agriculture, for trade, and to control population through dispersion of the people into adjacent areas. Over the lifetime of Nephi the people could have colonized many mountain valleys near by, and over the ensuing centuries the whole area would have cities built up according to the population growth, which would have been considerable over that time span.

City of Nephi at the time of King Noah

The City of Nephi was no doubt beautiful and was extremely desirable for Zeniff to have such a strong desire to return to the city from the strong hold of Zarahemla. The risk that Zeniff took knowing that the city was in the hands of the Lamanites makes one wonder why Zeniff and his people would want to return so badly. The City of Nephi must have been located in an area that was both extremely beautiful in scenery and climate or why would Zeniff have coveted the city so badly that he would have made such a pact with the enemy. It had to be a city worthy of taking the risk. For an agrarian society it had to be a city located in an area where the people could support themselves easily through their efforts to grow crops and herds. The Book of Mormon says that Zeniff made a covenant with King Laman to obtain the land:

> 7. "And he also commanded that his people should depart out of the land, and I and my people went into the land that we might possess it.
>
> 8. and we began to build buildings, and to repair the walls of the city, yea, even the walls of the city of Lehi-Nephi, and the city of Shilom.
>
> 9. And we began to till the ground, yea, even with all manner of seeds, with seeds of corn, and of wheat, and of barley, and with

Picture #27 A view of the city from the fortress on top of the hill.

146 CHARACTERISTICS OF THE CITY OF NEPHI

neas, and with sheum, and with seeds of all manner of fruits; and we did begin to multiply and prosper in the land." Mosiah 9:7-9

During the reign of Zeniff's son, the wicked King Noah, the city reaches its zenith on the heavily taxed backs of the people. The wicked king and his priests were the cause of many vain and extravagant buildings being built:

> 8. "And it came to pass that king Noah built many elegant and spacious buildings; and he ornamented them with fine work of wood, and of all manner of precious things, of gold, and of silver, and of iron, and of brass, and of ziff, and of copper;
> 9. And he also built him a spacious palace, and a throne in the midst thereof, all of which was of fine wood and was ornamented with gold and silver and with precious things.
> 10. And he also caused that his workmen should work all manner of fine work within the walls of the temple, of fine wood, and of copper, and of brass.
> 8. And it came to pass that he built a tower near the temple; yea, a very high tower, even so high that he could stand upon the top thereof and overlook the land of Shilom, and also the land of Shemlon, which was possessed by the Lamanites; and he could even look over all the land round about.
> 9. And it came to pass that he caused many buildings to be built in the land of Shilom, which had been a resort for the children of Nephi at the time they fled out of the land; and thus he did do with the riches which he obtained by the taxation of his people." Mosiah 11:8-10 & 12-13

During this time we find that the city now has many elegant and spacious buildings as well as a spacious palace. Another interesting feature is the appearance of very high outlook towers, both in the city proper and also in Shilom.

THE CITY OF NEPHI 147

Picture #28
Several places can be seen where presumably the ancient tunnel entrances surface.

The Fortress of Shilom

The hillside fortress of Shilom is also very important because it was a resort for the people to go to when they were in danger or under attack as we find out in verse 13.

So, this fortress of Shilom had huge walls that were repaired when Zeniff first returned and later towers and other buildings were built at this refuge or fortress that was to protect the people of the City of Nephi.

Secret Back Pass or Tunnels

The 'Secret Back Pass' or tunnels that connected the City of Nephi with Shilom and the fortress is also another important attribute of the City of Nephi. Shilom also plays an important role in the escape of the people from the Lamanites when Gideon presents his plan to King Limhi:

6. "Behold the back pass, through the back wall, on the back side of the city. The Lamanites, or the guards of the Lamanites, by night are drunken; therefore let us send a proclamation among all this people that they gather together their flocks and herds, that they may drive them into the wilderness by night.

7. And I will go according to thy command and pay the last tribute of wine to the Lamanites, and they will be drunken; and we will pass through the secret pass on the left of their camp when they are drunken and asleep.

8. Thus we will depart with our women and our children, our flocks, and our herds into the wilderness; and we will travel around the land of Shilom." Mosiah 22:6-8

Nephi was well acquainted with Jerusalem and the tunnel of Hezekiah that led from the temple mount within the walls of the city to the outside which was used in defence of the city and to be able to get water and provisions into the city during a siege. No doubt Nephi planned such defences and strategies for his city to connect it to the fortress of Shilom with a secret pass or tunnel. This pass could be used to move men and supplies to the refuge undetected and in this case to flee the city undetected by the Lamanites.

Lamanite City of Shemlon

Shemlon was a Lamanite city where the Lamanites could live near the City of Nephi to watch over them and keep track of the Nephites and extract their taxes from them. In Shemlon there was a place where the daughters of the Lamanites came to sing and dance and make merry. Where better to do that than at a pool of water or spring where they could wash and clean their clothes at a secluded spot away from the city. In Nephi's day this could have been a ceremonial center for baptisms and other functions which required the fountains and beautiful secluded pools of water. This is where the wicked priests of King Noah stole the daughters of the Lamanites:

1. "Now there was a place in Shemlon where the daughters of the Lamanites did gather themselves together to sing, and to dance, and to make themselves merry.

2. And it came to pass that there was one day a small number of them gathered together to sing and to dance. Mosiah 20:1-2

The City of Nephi after King Limhi

The City of Nephi remained an important capital city for many generations of Lamanite kings after the Nephites left the city. From about 90 to 77 B.C. the sons of Mosiah taught the Lamanites the gospel as missionaries. Ammon went to the Land of Middoni and taught the people of King Lamoni. Aaron went to the King of all the Lamanite lands, the father of Lamoni, even up unto the Land of Nephi and the City of Nephi, the capitol. The account in the Book of Mormon says:

1. "Now, as Ammon was thus teaching the people of Lamoni continually, we will return to the account of Aaron and his brethren; for after he departed from the land of Middoni he was led by the Spirit to the land of Nephi, even to the house of the king which was over all the land save it were the land of Ishmael; and he was the father of Lamoni.

2. And it came to pass that he went in unto him into the king's palace, with his brethren, and bowed himself before the king,….." Alma 21:1-2

One can clearly see that the City of Nephi still maintained its status as the capitol and it was where the king over all the land lived even under the occupation of the Lamanites. During the battles that Captain Moroni had with the Lamanites and Amalickiah in 72 B.C., the City of Nephi is mentioned when Lehonti dies. Amalickiah marches on the city to take over as King of the Lamanites:

20. "And it came to pass that Amalickiah marched with his armies (for he had gained his desires) to the land of Nephi, to the city of Nephi, which was their chief city." Alma 47:20

The city of Nephi was the chief city of the Lamanites, and it is mentioned one last time in the Book of Mormon. In about 30 B.C. the sons of Helaman, Nephi and Lehi, preach and convert most of the Nephites and then start teaching the Lamanites as well. The Book of Mormon records:

20. "And it came to pass that Nephi and Lehi did proceed from thence to go to the land of Nephi.

21. And it came to pass that they were taken by an army of the Lamanites and cast into prison; yea, even in that same prison in which Ammon and his brethren were cast by the servants of Limhi," Helaman 5:20-21

This prison was in the capitol city of Nephi, and evidently it was still in use. Nephi and Lehi went to the City of Nephi because it was the capitol of the Lamanites and where the king lived and their most important city. Here they were able to convert the Lamanites.

It is interesting that during the massive destructions during the Coming of Christ to the Americas that the City of Nephi is not mentioned and is presumably left unharmed from the earthquakes and volcanic eruptions that devastated so many other cities. There is afterwards a shift to the land northward where the Nephite culture migrated and fighting with the Lamanites occurred until the end of the Book of Mormon. The rest of the account of the Book of Mormon focuses on the activity of the Nephites north of the narrow neck of land, and Mormon and Moroni never have cause to mention the Land of Nephi again in their writings.

Towers in the Land of Nephi

One of the most important features of the City of Nephi and surrounding cities and lands is that the Nephites constructed towers as part of the defence facilities of their cities. Very tall towers gave them the advantages of having look-outs on duty to spot enemies in advance. This advance notice gave them the ability to avoid any surprise attacks by the Lamanites. Towers were built next to the temple in the City of Nephi. Towers were also built in the city of Shimlon and at the fortress on the north of the city of Shimlon. These towers were mentioned several times in the Book of Mormon and were no doubt an important archaeological feature of Nephi's city for us in modern times to discover. We summarize this chapter with a Brief History and 16 Characteristics of the City of Nephi found below.

A Brief Summary of the History of the City of Nephi

- Founded by Nephi in a virgin, non-populated land approx. 590-580 B.C.

- Built city and a temple and lived there until King Mosiah I moved people to Zarahemla in 205-200B.C. (approx. 390 Years)
- The City of Nephi was vacant for awhile and occupied by Lamanites.
- King Zeniff returned to City of Nephi in approximately 200B.C., the Nephites lived there until 121 B.C. City and walls were rebuilt, many new buildings were built. Total Nephite Era (approx. 450 years)
- From 121 B.C. it became the Capitol City of the Lamanites until the coming of Jesus Christ.
- Ammon's brother, Aaron, taught King Laman and converted the Lamanites in the City of Nephi from 90-77 B.C.
- Not mentioned again after Christ in the Book of Mormon.

There are at least 16 characteristics of the City of Nephi that are paramount to any archeological, geological, and geographic study of the Book of Mormon. They are:

The 16 Characteristics of the City of Nephi
1. Legends of founding of the City – Founder, People, & Virgin Land
2. Historical Capitol City of many Cultures
3. High Towers at Temple and Resort
4. Temple built after the manner of Solomon.
5. Temple is the center point or focal point of the city. 4 Quadrants
6. Temple of Nephi had beautiful gardens.
7. Lower or older portion of City of Nephi. Two Constructions
8. Upper or newer portion is City of Shilom.
9. Defensive resort associated with City.
10. City of Nephi was a walled city.
11. Lamanite City nearby called Shemlon.
12. Lamanite Baths or place of rest.
13. Agricultural bread basket to support millions of people.
14. Immense treasure city and temple. King Noah adorned it.
15. City located in an area where there was gold for making plates for record keeping. Minerals for making metal for all useful implements.
16. A back pass or secret passage way.

Summary of the City of Nephi

A good description of the City of Nephi can be formulated from the Book of Mormon and the little hints that are found in the scriptures. We have discussed the type of city that Nephi, the prophet, was likely to build with its nice stone buildings and beautiful streets all laid out in perfect order and with the guidance from God to his prophet. To fit the scriptural account the City of Nephi would have to be: a walled city with very high towers, a city with secret passage ways or tunnels, a city with an old and a newer section, a city with fountains and rivers, a city with a history of being the 'chief' or capitol city of the empire, and finally a city that was beautiful both in climate and scenery. The temple would be the main focal point in his city. The temple would be at the center with the streets and the city radiating out in all directions from the temple in four quadrants. It would have been the navel and the center of Nephi's universe. The city would have to be in an area where even if there were earthquakes and calamities they would not have affected the overall construction of the city for centuries as per the scriptural account. The need for protection for the city and its people would necessitate building a resort or fortress against attack from the Lamanites. So, the neighboring city of Shilom with its fortress or resort and high towers were an important attribute of the City and Land of Nephi. The city went through continuous growth for 390 years and then a remodelling during the Zeniff to Limhi period, so in essence two distinct construction periods. It is fair to say that the City of Nephi became a great city that was the chief city or capitol city of many civilizations down through the centuries to the present day. From the scriptures we can readily visualize this city and the surrounding areas that became the home of Nephi and his people, the Nephites.

{Facing Picture for Ch #8} The focal point or jewel of the City of Cusco was the sacred temple.

CHAPTER 8

CITY OF CUSCO, PERU

Pre-Inca Civilization

To really research the beginnings of the City of Cusco, the center of civilization in South America, we must get some background on the peoples that lived here. We must look at the various types of archaeology and stone construction, art, time periods, and culture. Then we will compare the city of Cusco with what we know about the City of Nephi. We will discover that Cusco has all of the characteristics of the ancient capitol of the Nephites.

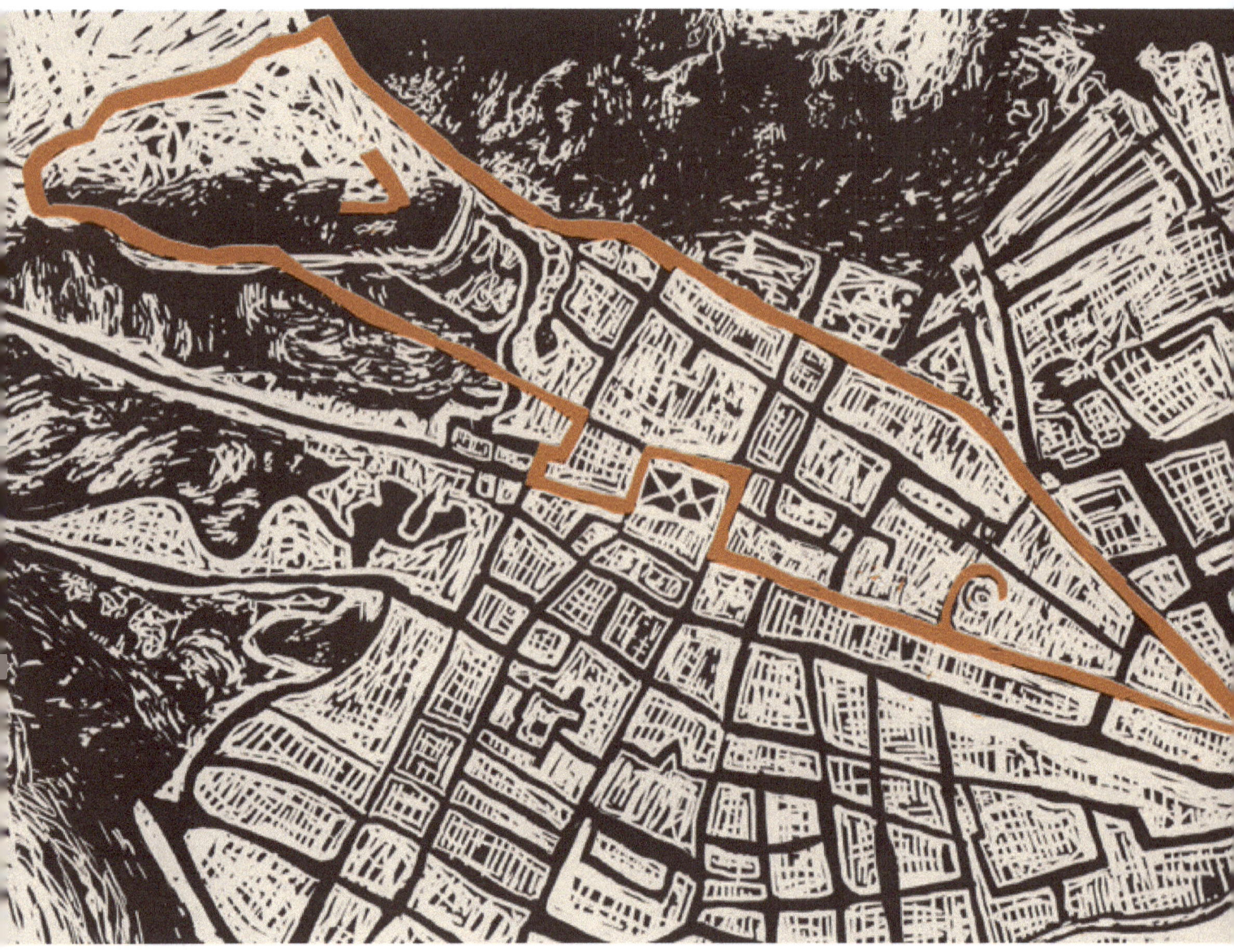

Picture #29
The ancient city of Cusco was built in the form of a Puma (Cougar or Mountain Lion). The top of the head was the Fortress of Sacsahuaman, the neck was the neck was the Plaza de Armas and the navel was the Temple of Koricancha and the three rivers of Cusco converge to form the tail.

Cusco was discovered and constructed anciently, and has been continuously populated to modern times. Most archeologists place the founding of Cusco and attribute the construction of the city to the Chavin Culture in approximately 600BC. Some recent scientists say that it could have been populated even earlier. According to Dr. Keith Tankard, "Cusco was first occupied by the Chavin people (900-200 BC), the Tiahuanacan Dynasty (600-1000 AD), and then the Inca Empire (1476-1534 AD). Ref 18. The Olmec or Jaredite time period is approximately 2200 BC and doesn't really concern the City of Nephi and this book because their cultures never coincide or interact during the Nephite Era. There are however, ruins of great Olmec civilizations in Peru and South America just not in the Cusco area. Time periods can vary greatly between the experts, according to the many scientists and archaeologists involved in their many individual studies. It is a difficult procedure at best, to use dating systems.

156 CITY OF CUSCO, PERU

Figure #24 Modern day map of the city of Cusco, Peru, showing the bisecting lines of the ancient tunnels underneath the city that are not accessible to the public, yet.

Can you imagine trying to date the Temple of Koricancha for example using samples of stone that existed from the beginning of time with no man-made mortar or cement between the joints. Dating methods and dating technology vary and causes diversity in interpretation. All scientists realize that absolute truth is quite difficult to nail down given man's finite skills, even as the methods and technology get better over time. Carbon dating has never been an exact science. It is only as good as the samples and methodology used.

So, it is easier for us and more accurate in the opinion of LDS scholars to establish the time period from the Book of Mormon for the City of Nephi as 590 - 580 B.C. to 130 B.C. as the Nephite Era, about 130 B.C. to 1400 AD as the Lamanite Era (Aymara and Quechua speaking natives), and then finally the Inca Empire or Quechua speaking natives from around about 1200-1400 AD to 1534 AD. The Inca Empire was followed by the Spanish Colonial Era from 1534 AD to about 1821 AD and liberation from Spanish Rule by Jose de San Martin. The Modern Period we will call from 1821 AD to the Present. Very interesting side note is that the Modern Period of South America coincides exactly with the restoration of the gospel in the latter days and the prophet Joseph Smith. In fact you can rightly say that the Lord has been preparing this land and this people to receive the restored gospel for centuries that one day it may 'blossom like a rose', again.

Cusco has been continuously populated and occupied since the first Chavin people or Nephites arrived in 590 B.C. Each conquering civilization or culture has built upon the older civilization and left their

Picture #30
View of the modern city of Cusco from the Fortress of Sacsahuaman.

mark on the city. Each culture has adopted or borrowed many things from the previous group and integrated them into their own unique culture. Many of the Spanish conquistadors for instance married Inca women 'Coyas' and had their own unique brand of Catholicism which became a blend of Inca and Spanish traditions. Many conquistadors actually joined in marrying a 'Coya' as a surrogate wife, or proxy for their legal spouse back in Spain. The Incas borrowed many of the legends and traditions of the Chavin people such as the legend of Manco Capac to make them more powerful and their culture and kings immortal in their memories.

The Chavin Culture

If the Chavin people are the actual Nephite civilization then it requires a closer study. This important discussion describes at length the similarities between what we know about the Nephites and what the world knows about the Chavin Culture.

> "At regular intervals through the centuries, brilliant all-conquering civilizations arose on the (Andean) Cordillera. Thus, more than 500 years before Christ, the culture of Chavin emerged in the central Andes and extended its influence as far as the coast." Ref 14 *The Incas – Empire of Blood and Gold* by Carmen Bernand p.23

These people were the first apparently to inhabit the land of Cusco and presumably built this magnificent city. The Chavin people are said to have been pale skinned and large in stature.

> "The Chavins built citadels (fortresses), *pucara*, throughout the empire. The most majestic fortress, that of Sacsahuaman still overlooks the town of Cusco. It is surrounded by a wall of stones that are so well fitted that a knife-blade cannot be inserted between them. It was defended, in Inca times, by three towers which communicated with the Inca's palace (and temple) by underground passages….The people of Cuzco referred to their empire as the 'Land of the Four Quarters', Tahuantinsuyu, a name that was both symbolic and administrative: the empire was arranged around Cuzco, the 'naval', in four great sectors orientated to the cardinal points. To the north stretched Chinchaysuyu; to the south Collasuyu, where the Lupaqa lords of Lake Titicaca lived; Cuntisuyu extended westwards; and, finally Antisuyu opened on the Amazonian piedmont,…." Ref 14 *The Incas – Empire of Blood and Gold* by Carmen Bernand p.22-23

The Chavin people have a very distinct culture and are known for their expertise in stone work and building, for their farming and terracing, and for their art and weaving. These are so many of the same traits that Nephi instilled in his little group of followers. Below is a quote regarding the Chavin culture:

> "The Chavin culture is known for its beautiful art and design but Chavin was also innovative with metallurgy and textile production. Cloth production was revolutionized during the time of Chavin. New techniques and materials are popular through the use of camel hair, textile painting, the dying of camel hair and the 'resist' painting style similar to modern day tie-dye. Advances in metallurgy also occurred during the Chavin's reign in Peru such as joining pieces of preshaped metal sheets to form both objects of art and objects for practical use. Soldering and temperature control were also advanced during this time.
>
> An important factor of the Chavin culture is its art, which can seem very puzzling to the untrained eye. Chavin designs can be appreciated only as abstract patterns, but there is almost always representational meaning behind them. Chavin art bears some resemblance to Olmec art suggesting that there may have been some degree of influence between the two cultures." Ref 19. Soustelle, Jacques. *The Route of the Incas*. The Viking Press, New York.

The Chavin civilization has got to be the focus of any Book of Mormon study comparative with the ancient Nephites. The Nephites were a large, white race of people that were organized into a structured agrarian society as was the Chavin culture. They built buildings, roads, fortresses, and irrigation canals in similar manner. Another noted writer about ancient Andean cultures, Dr. Keith Tankard, has this to say about the Chavin people:

> "Chavin culture (named after the town where the most important archaeological site has been found), was based in the Peruvian Andes, and flourished from 1500 to 300 BC. Surviving artefacts include stone sculpture. The Chavin people, the first "civilization" of South America, had a major influence on the cultures that followed it. They appear to be the ancestors of the Aymara speaking peoples of the Andes. While the Chavin culture dominated the Peruvian highlands, culturally distinct societies were developing on the north coast of Peru. These people were probably from the other major language group of western South

America, Quechua. Metallurgy had been established since at least 2100 BC.

Stone sculpture - The highly stylized form of this jaguar was typical of Chavin art. It is based on a bas relief stone sculpture. The colours are not known for sure, but are based on ancient textiles. Much other art from South and Central America shows use of stylized forms.

The Andean culture differed from the Meso-American variety in three specific ways. First, while the Meso-Americans domesticated no beast of burden, the Andean peoples did, in the form of the llama and the alpaca (both camelids). The former were used as pack animals, while the latter were more specifically for food and wool. Since neither was suitable for pulling, the Andean peoples had therefore no use for the wheel.

The Andean peoples were also much more advanced as technicians and engineers. Metallurgy was better developed and put to more practical uses. They were also more advanced in road and canal building, being able to span deep gorges with their bridges. Their statecraft too was more highly developed, although they lagged behind in the development of writing.

Although the basic Andean cultural patterns were probably set as early as 2000 BC, there were nevertheless three distinct eras in their evolution: the Chavin people (900-200 BC), the Tiahuanacan Dynasty (600-1000 AD) and the Inca Empire (1476-1534 AD).

Very little is known about the Chavin Dynasty except that it had its centre in the ruins called Chavin de Huantar, a religious site in the Andes. The people had already reached the highest level of artistry, and their forms of pottery are found in a wide area of Peru.

The Chavin era ended in about 200 BC and was replaced by what is known as an intermediate period during which a variety of regional cultures flourished for a period of about 800 years." Ref 18. Dr. Keith Tankard, The Inca Empire – S.A. Labrinth

Cusco has long been considered the cradle of civilization for South America. This city interestingly is void of any pyramids, but does have a beautiful stone temple once adorned with gold and silver. It is revered even today as the center of their ancient religion and the capital of the ancient civilization.

MODERN CUSCO

THE MEANING OF THE WORD CUSCO comes from the Quechua word **QOSQO** which means navel, it has quite a few meanings, one of the most important is **"Center or navel of the world"** which was given by the famous cusquenian writer Inka Garcilaso de la Vega.

>> **LOCATION:** The department of Cusco is located in the south east region of the Peruvian Andes, at 72° 00 away from west of the Greenwich meridian timeline.

>> **AREA:** The department of Cusco has an area of 76,225 Km² and the province of Cusco has an area of 523 Km².

>> **ALTITUDE:** Cusco is located at 3350 meter above the sea level measured from the Main Square of Cusco.

>> **WEATHER:** It is quite cold and dry, it has two clearly noticeable seasons: the rainy season from November to March, when the temperature rises from 11°C to 13°C. And the dry season from April to October, with particular sunny days and very cold nights, the temperature stays only an average of 9°C.

Cusco and the Surrounding Area

The Land of Nephi or the city and the surrounding area are very important to our study. Although we do not know a lot about the 'Land of Nephi' from the scriptures we do know that it became intensely populated over the centuries. At the height of the Incan Civilization, historians have recorded that the population could have reached upwards of fifteen million inhabitants within the empire. Cusco, the Sacred Valley, Ollantaytambo, Machu Pichu, and other cities are close enough together to actually be part of the 'Land of Nephi'. A nice five day hike along the famous Inca Trail will reward the traveler a view of many cities and ruins that are inaccessible by modern vehicles.

Incan Roads

In the Surrounding Cusco area there are a lot of evidences of the ancient Incan roads that were most likely started during the Chavin era. These roads are engineering marvels even today. They connect all of the main cities and way stations. Their construction most certainly took a great deal of energy and manpower for this civilization before the machinery of our modern technology. The provisions for drainage, erosion control, and earthquake resistance makes the survival of these roads even more of a modern day miracle.

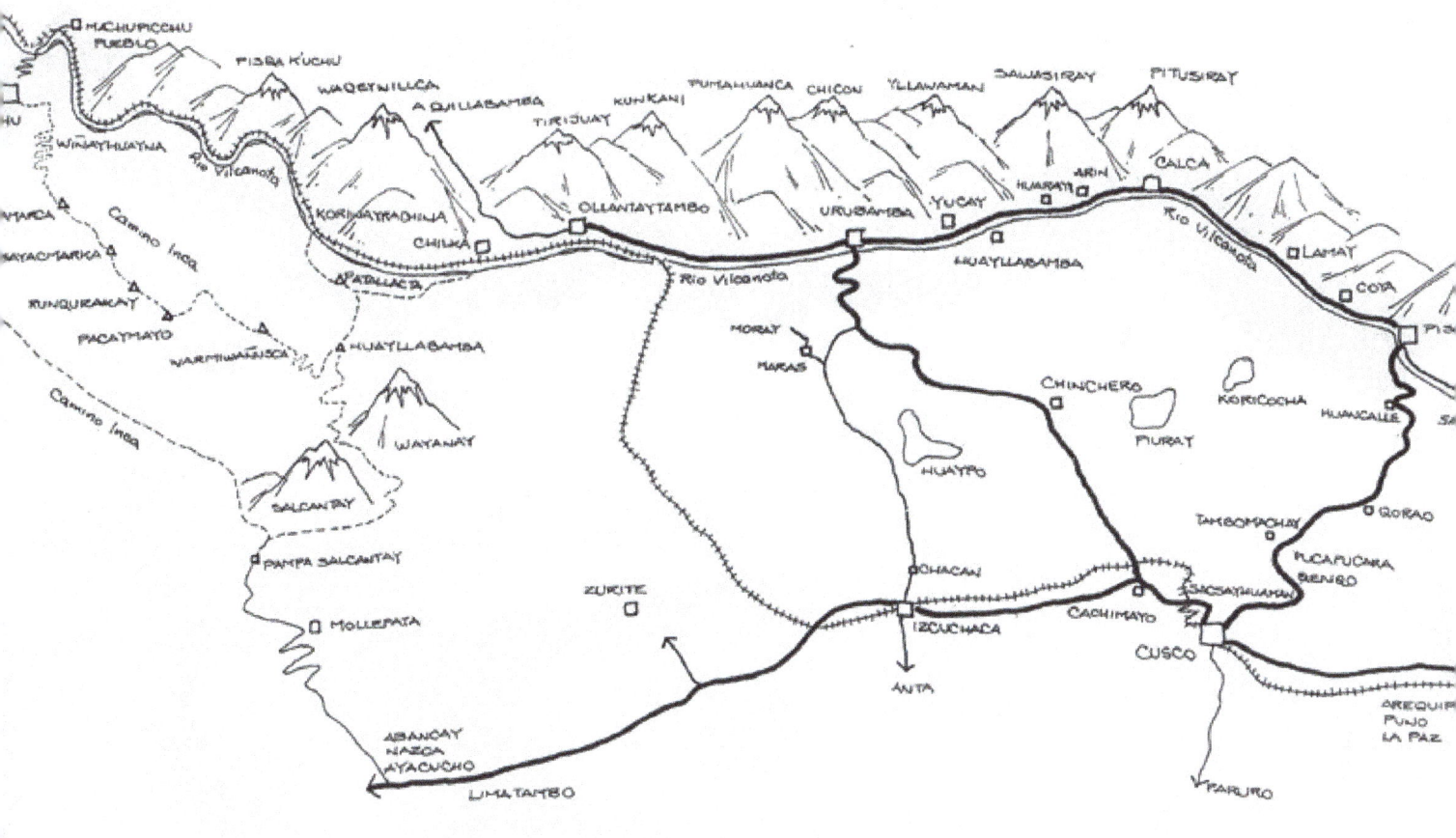

Figure #25 A schematic drawing of the famed Inca Trail and its ruined cities.

Main Buildings of Cusco City Center

In the following discussion, we will name several of the main temples and palaces of the ancient city and give directions and places to where the Spanish built Churches and other structures over these main Inca buildings.

Even though the Inca history tends to begin with the Inca Pachacuteq's or Pachacuti's period (the one who made the earth spin) In 1438, the Inka empire reached its best time. Pachacutec wasn't only a great warrior he was also a great leader who could reorganize the Inka society and the city of Cusco itself. This development got a little bit better when Wayna Capac rose up as the new Inka in 1493, and finally went down when the Spanish invaded their territory. The Spaniards, Pizarro's small army, arrived in Cusco on November 15th, 1533. Pedro Del Barco and Hernando De Soto were the first to set foot in the ancient capital of Cusco in a forward scouting patrol. These two brave conquistadors gave the first account of

THE CITY OF NEPHI 163

Picture #31
Inca Road that is part of the famous 'Inca Trail' between Cusco and Machu Pichu.

'El Dorado' and the Temple of Gold that glistened in the setting sun, (The Temple of Koricancha).

The urban aspect of Cusco changed a lot after their arrival, they built churches, casonas, and palaces over the main Icka temples, and only the Spanish were allowed to occupy them. And finally an earthquake in 1650 finished with the transformation of this once-great-empire.

QASANA

Group of Buildings which where on the south east side reach the Wacaypata (today Plaza de Armas), it was the palace of the Inka Pachacutec and residence of the elite Iñapa Panaka Ayllu.

It was handed to Francisco Pizarro during the first distribution of palaces and cult houses.

>> **MEANING OF THE WORD:** The word Qasana mean "Icy Place" or "where the frost falls".

>> **LOCATION:** It was located where nowadays we know as Portal de Panes, and once inside you could have been able to find your way to the School Neighbourhood. The palace went along the Saphy River and one of the sides was connected to the palace of Qoraqora.

QORAQORA

This palace was built under the order of Inca Roca and was the residence of the ayllu Raurau, during the distribution of territories Gonzalo Pizarro took this palace under his possession.

>> **MEANING OF THE WORD:** Qoraqora means Herb Field or Place with abundant plants.

>> **LOCATION:** Located at the north-west side of Qasana, originally these were two connected residences, nowadays they are separated by the Procuradores St. It is located in what we know now as Portal de Harinas, The east side of the palace was connected to Suecia street.

KISWAR KANCHA

It had many inside buildings, it belonged to the Inka Wiraccocha and had a particular rectangle shape, and it was also the residence of Sujsu Ayllu. When the Spanish took possession of the palaces this one was given to Alonzo de Meza.

>> **MEANING OF THE NAME:** Kiswar means: native bush; pretty much like the Alamo, the whole name is translated as Kisware's place.

>> **LOCATION:** It is located on the north-east side of the Wacaypata (Plaza de Armas), exactly where the Cathedral and the Sacred Family Temple are located.

SUNTUR WASI

In the Inka times it was considered the House of the Weapons and Troffees, It had a cylindrical shape and had several floors. When the Spanish arrived, Pizarro ordered that this temple was meant to be the first Spanish Catholic Church in Cusco.

> **MEANING OF THE WORD:** This word means house of the Condor.
> **LOCATION:** It was part of the Kiswar Cancha, on the south side; this area is now occupied by the Triunfo Church.

HATUN KANCHA

It was built under the orders of Inca Yupanqui, that's where his Panaca lived.
> **MEANING OF THE WORD:** It means great Fence.
> **LOCATION:** It used to be located on what we know now as Triunfo, Santa Catalina and Herrajes streets.

AJLLA WASI

In the Inka Times there was this huge house where they use to host the chosen virgins; this house had only cult and religious purposes. When the Spanish arrived this place was given to Francisco Mejía, Pedro de Barco, and to some other Spaniards. Afterwards the Ajlla Wasi was converted into a Convent mostly known as Convento de Santa Catalina.
> **MEANING OF THE WORD:** It means House of the Chosen Women
> **LOCATION:** It was located between the streets Santa Catalina, Arequipa and Loreto. The west side of the temple was connected to the Waqaypata and the east side to the Maruri Street.

AMARU KANCHA

This was an enormous group of buildings built under the order of Wayna Qapaj, it was also the residence of Tumipampa Ayllu. Once the Spanish invaded Cusco these temples were given to Hernando Pizarro, Manzo Sierra de Leguizamo, Antonio Altamirano and Alonzo Mazuela. Afterwards it was occupied by the Jesuits who built the actual Church of La Compañia de Jesus.
> **MEANING OF THE WORD:** Amaru means: Snake and Kancha means: field.
> **LOCATION:** Located between the Loreto streets and Sol Avenue, its west side was connected to the Waqaypata and the east side was connected to the Afligidos Street.

QORICANCHA

This was the most important temple of all in Cusco; it was dedicated to the cult of their God Sun (Inti), and also to the cult of some minor Gods. Nowadays the Convent of Santo Domingo is located over this Inka Temple. Also, known as the Temple of Koricancha

>> **MEANING OF THE WORD:** It means golden House.

>> **LOCATION:** It is located on the Plazoleta of Santo Domingo.

QOLLQANPATA

It was a very important neighbourhood in Inka times, inside this palace there were some houses which are important for two particular reasons: The palace of the same name and the adoring Huaca or temple of Sapantiana. It is well known that this palace belonged to the Inka Manco Capac; this was the best located palace in Cusco. When the Spaniards arrived this place was given to Diego de Almagro and was handed afterwards to the Church of San Cristóbal.

>> **MEANING OF THE WORD:** It means deposit..

>> **LOCATION:** It is located down the Sacsahuaman hill.

JATUNRUMIYUC

This palace was built by Inca Roca, the most important thing about this palace is the Lienzo pétreo which is a beautiful wall which bends backwards, and built out of dorita verde or green stone, here you will find the famous twelve-angle-rock. The whole palace was destroyed and the only part that remains perfect is this gorgeous wall.

>> **MEANING OF THE WORD:** Hatun means: house or temple, Rumiyuc means: big rock. So Jatunrumiyuc means Temple of Big Rock.

>> **LOCATION:** Taking as reference point the Plaza de Armas, go on towards the Church Triunfo, and we arrive at a street called Hatunruniyoc, where this palace is located.

PUKAMARCA or HATUN KANCHA

This palace belonged to Tupaq Inka Yupanqui, it was also the residence of his Panaca called Hatun Ayllu.

>> **MEANING OF THE WORD:** It means Red Palace, because it has been built with red stone.

>> **LOCATION:** Its location is between the following streets Maruri, San Agustín, Santa Catalina and Arequipa.

The Incan Dynasty

According to the Spanish Chronicler, Garcilaso de la Vega, Manco Capac was the first Inca and he established the city of Cusco as their home. He comments:

> "While peopling the city, our Inca taught the male Indians the tasks that were to be theirs, such as selecting seeds and tilling the soil. He taught them how to make hoes, how to irrigate their fields by means of canals that connected natural streams, and even to make these same shoes that we still wear today. The queen, meanwhile, was teaching the women how to spin and weave wool and cotton, how to make clothing, as well as other domestic tasks. In short, our sovereigns, the Inca king, who was master of the men, and Queen Coya, who was mistress of the women, taught their subjects everything that had to do with human living…..He had taught them to make bows, lances, arrows, and bludgeons… Such then,…were the beginnings of our city which, today, as you can see, is rich and populous; …..And such were our first Incas, our first kings, those who came here during the first centuries of the world and from whom all our other kings are descended,….. Our Inca's name was Manco Capac and our Coya Mama, Occlo Huaco." Ref 3. p. 7-8

There is a tremendous similarity with the succession of kings here between the Inca Empire and the Book of Mormon. As previously discussed the kings in the Book of Mormon were named First Nephi, Second Nephi, and so on. In the Incan tradition they also numbered their kings and the associated dynasty.

> "There was a succession of twelve Inca dynasties at Cusco; the thirteenth Inca being Atahualpa…..The number of Inca dynasties and their historical reality are a matter of debate. According to the best established theory, there were five Incas belonging to the Hurin dynasty and eight other sovereigns belonging to the Hanan dynasty, which was hierarchically superior. The emperor or Sapa Inca was himself the son of the Sun and was worshipped as such.". *The Incas – Empire of Blood and Gold* by Carmen Bernand p.23-25.

During the 1520's, the great Inca king was Huayna Capac (Eleventh Inca in the Dynasty). At this time Pizarro scouted and explored the coasts of Ecuador and Peru and learned of the Inca Empire. The Inca king also learned of the Spaniards and died of their smallpox disease without ever having met one. Huayna Capac, however, did have a dream and prophesied about the white bearded men that would bring peace and a new government to his land. He believed that the time had come for Wiracochan to return as the ancient prophecies had foretold and preached this concept to his people.

Pizarro returned to Spain in 1528 to enlist the financial help of the Spanish Crown that he needed in conquering Peru. During this time of absence the legitimate son Huascar warred against his half-brother Atahualpa, the illegitimate son. The kingdom split in two with Huascar being made king of Cusco, Peru and Atahualpa king of Quito, Ecuador, the Inca's second capital. Atahualpa supporters later eventually assassinated Huascar and he claimed the empire for himself. Pizarro arrived back from Spain in the middle of this intense civil war and confusion. The Inca Empire was an easy prey for the bearded white men traveling on the water's foam in white sailing ships with their thunder guns and shinning armor. Francisco Pizarro was thought to be Wiracochan returning to save his people. Francisco Pizarro was given control of the Incan Capital City, Cusco, without any kind of battle what so ever. Francisco married the Inca Huayna Capac's daughter, Lacoya Ines, and governed Cusco in peace for several years. Pizarro was hailed as Wiracochan, the Son of God, who would come and establish peace and his kingdom in the last days according to the prophecies and legends of the Inca people. He had come in like manner as when he had left centuries before.

Picture #32
Famous painting of Francisco Pizarro, first governor of Peru.

THE CITY OF NEPHI

Cusco – The Center

The center of the Empire and civilization for the Incas, the Aymara and Quechua peoples, and the Chavin race has always been Cusco. In fact it was in deed the very heart of their government, their capitol and most important city, the hub of their commerce and markets, and most importantly the center of their religion. Of course the kings and Incas that controlled Cusco ruled generally all of South America.

It was the city of kings and religious leaders that governed their society. Cusco has always been considered by the Incas as the center of the universe, the navel of the world. The Inca tradition is that it is shaped in the form of a puma (mountain lion) with the temple as the navel. Garcilaso de la Vega said of Cusco:

> "The Inca kings divided the Empire into four districts, according to the cardinal points, the whole of which they called *Tahuantinsuyu*, which means the four parts of the world. The center was Cusco which, in the Peruvian language, means the navel of the world. This name was well chosen, since Peru is long and narrow like the human body, and Cusco is situated in the middle of the belly." Ref 3. p18.

Figure #26
Cusco was built in the form of a Puma with: E) The Head, Sacsahuaman C) The neck, Plaza de Armas D) The Navel, Koricancha Temple A) Male parts B) The Tail or convergence of the three rivers of Cusco.

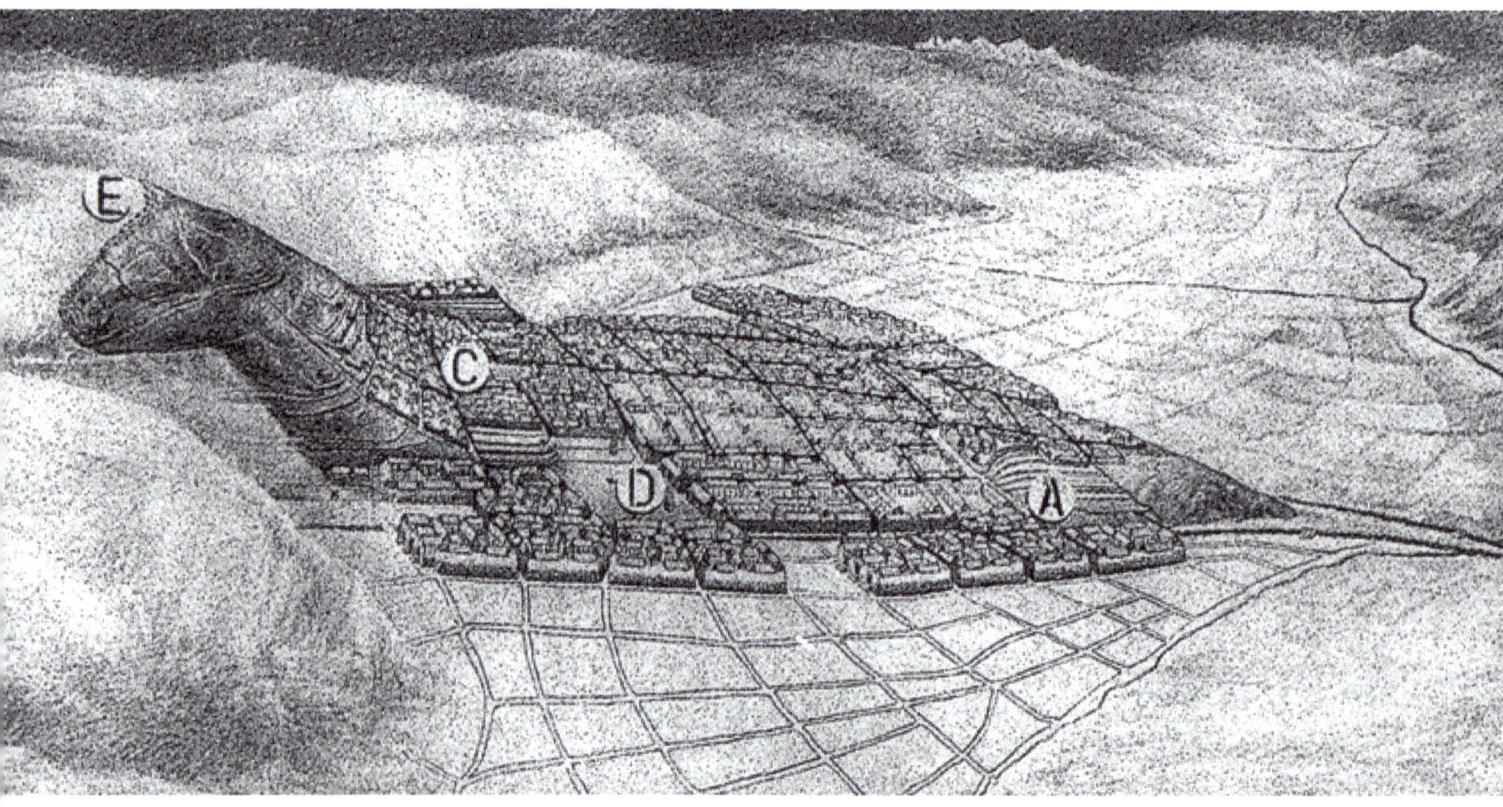

170   CITY OF CUSCO, PERU

Pre-Columbian Era

It will be important to take a look at Cusco through the eyes of the Spanish Chroniclers and ancient 'rememberers' as much as possible to visualize how Cusco was before Pizarro and his conquistadors first reached this Inca capital. Cusco is a city that has been continually occupied by various peoples since the Nephites built it in 585 B.C. It is nestled in a high altitude valley of the Andes Mountains at 11,000 ft above sea level. At the time of Pizarro and the conquistadors in 1533, Cusco was the capitol of the Inca Empire that was embroiled in a terrible civil war between brothers for the kingdom. The Inca Empire was already on the decline from its zenith and found itself in a vulnerable situation when the Spanish came to conquer this land. This is a description of what Cusco was like by the first of the Chroniclers:

Pizarro and the Spaniards

When Hernando de Soto and Pedro Del Barco, another Spanish conquistador who were part of an advance group of Francisco Pizarro's army, first viewed the city of Cusco from a far off in the early evening, they saw the Temple of Koricancha glistening with the setting sun rays. The astonished soldiers knew that they had finally found their golden city, the 'Eldorado' that they had been searching for. Pizarro entered the Inca capital on November 15th 1533 and immediately took control of the city without any resistance. The conquerors were impressed with the lavish stone buildings and palaces and the temple with its high tower. They were impressed with the Fortress of Sacsahuaman and its towers. In the end they were mostly impressed with the quantity of gold and silver treasure. Diego de Almagro was Francisco Pizarro's partner in the conquest and was in charge of transporting supplies. Almagro had been cut out of the dispersion of treasure from Cajamarca because he was not present at the battle. So, this time Almagro was intent on getting what was rightfully due to him and his men. The personal conflict between these two conquerors would become the source of a civil war between the conquistadors and cause much bloodshed. Eventually, the greed and hatred would destroy both of them. Cusco was indeed the prize that the conquistadors had dreamed about. They amalgamated an immense treasure as they ransacked the palaces and public places. Over seven hundred panels of gold were extracted from the walls of the Temple or Koricancha along with many other beautiful gold and silver artefacts. The treasure was so immense that it made Atahualpa's ransom treasure of one room of gold and two rooms of silver in Cajamarca

Figure #27
Incas divided their Kingdom into four quarters with Cusco in the middle.

172 CITY OF CUSCO, PERU

dwarf in comparison. Only the king's fifth or twenty percent of the treasure and a little bit that a few conquistadors secreted away ever left Peru and made it back to Spain. The rest has remained in Peru to the present time, mostly hidden presumably. When Francisco Pizarro left Cusco in 1535 to go to establish his Peruvian capital in Lima, then Hernando Pizarro (Francisco's brother) was given charge of Cusco. Hernando waged several battles against Manco Capac II, the new Inca King, and the 'Men of Chile' (Army of Diego de Almagro). Hernando finally prevailed and executed Almagro for treason. What had at first been a peaceful conquest became a brutal series of battles for control over the capitol city, the prize of the Incan Empire. The Spanish conquistadors had a dispersal of properties in 1536 that was significant, wherein Hernando was given the Koricancha Temple property. Hernando left for Spain in 1538 with the king's fifth and was imprisoned on his arrival for twenty years for his execution of Almagro, (the governor of Chile could only be executed by the King of Spain. The Temple of Koricancha was later given to the Dominican priests who built their Santo Domingo Chapel over the top of the walls of the sacred Koricancha Temple. The chapel has been rebuilt three times over the last four hundred years because of earthquakes. The remaining walls of Koricancha were unaffected by the earthquakes.

Location of the Temple of Koricancha

Cusco is divided historically into two city areas Hanan-Cuzco and Huron-Cuzco. The lower city, Huron-Cuzco is thought to be the oldest part of the city, or our City of Nephi. The temple of Koricancha is located in the northern most part of the highest part of this part of the city. The Cusco valley is a long and wide valley that increases in elevation from 9,200 ft. to 10231 ft. as it ascends in elevation to the north with mountains encircling around it. The Temple of Koricancha is located exactly as the requirements with the Temple of Solomon. It is situated in the highest place of the most northern area of the city, literally at the tops of the mountains. The newer city of Hanan-Cuzco, or political center of wicked King Noah is centered approximately 10 blocks further north at the crest of the valley. This part of the city of Cusco being newer was probably built later by the wicked King Noah when he built many beautiful and spacious buildings. Today this is the center of Cusco city where the Main Cathedral, main city square (Plaza de Armas), and other important government buildings are located.

Picture #33
Plaza de Armas is the main city square of the city of Cusco, Peru.

The Fortress of Sacsahuaman

Probably the most impressive site of Pre-Columbian ruins anywhere in the Americas is the fortress or resort that protects the ancient city of Cusco. This colossal three-level fortress (citadel) spans more than 600 meters in a slightly concave line with buttresses jutting out at regular intervals. The first level or base of the fortress is six meters high with an entrance almost in the middle made of a beautiful fitted stone doorway which controlled passage. The second level is set back 20 meters from the first and is again an average of six meters high. The third level is set back about 18 meters and is approximately five meters high.

The massive walls of the fortress are built of huge Andesite stones estimated to weigh between 100 and 400 tons and fitted and carved so precisely that they have been able to withstand the centuries and several major earthquakes with no apparent damage. No mortar was used to bond them together, and yet a knife blade cannot be inserted between them. The Spanish Conquistadors were so impressed with this fortress that they could not believe that it was constructed by human hands. See photo #35.

Picture #34
The Fortress of Sacsahuaman situated on the north of Cusco, Peru.

Towers of Sacsahuaman

On top of the Sacsahuaman fortress there stands the remains of three huge towers. These towers were used strategically for defence as look-out towers, but had also a religious function as well. These towers were still present and functional during the Spanish Colonial era. Many Spanish Chroniclers commented on the impressive height of the towers as being taller than any in Seville, Spain. Over the centuries the stones have been stolen from the towers and only the foundations remain and are protected in our modern day by the national government.

The nobility or kings with their priests lived and used the towers and associated buildings and rooms for ceremonial and religious rites that were handed down through the centuries and used by each succeeding Inca king. These towers, and the Sacsahuaman fortress itself was connected to the underground passageway that led to Cusco and the Temple of Koricancha.

Picture #35
The massive fortress is more than six hundred meters in length.

Picture #36 This is the foundation of the great circular lookout tower at the Fortress of Sacsahuaman. Notice the stone water pipelines that circulated water to the facility.

Manner of Construction

The exquisite stone work in the construction of the buildings in Cusco was impressive to the Spaniards. They saw and recorded the impressive worked Andesite walls that fitted stones on top of each other without the aide of mortar. The work was so well accomplished that a knife blade could not be inserted between the joints of the individual worked rocks or dressed stone. The Spanish also noted that the Incan walls 'leaned' and started out measurably larger at the base as the walls coursed upward. This construction was impressive because it withstood the ages and the earthquakes predominant in the area. The stone masonry was really of the highest quality on all of the Incan palaces and buildings.

The Tunnels of Cusco

One of the most intriguing studies conducted recently in Peru in August 2000, was carried out in Cusco at the Temple of Koricancha by Spanish archaeologist, Anselm Pi Rambla called the Wiracocha Project. Using modern technology, a method called 'Ground Penetrating Radar' (GPR), a group of scientists from Spain called the 'Bohic Ruz Explorer' have been able to map out a system of tunnels that radiate out from the Temple of Koricancha. One entrance at the temple site appears to be beneath the altar of Santa Rosa, which is the main altar of the temple. This series of tunnels is five meters deep and is of ancient design. It extends from Koricancha to the Plaza de Armas and then to the fortress of Sacsahuaman some two kilometers in length. The tunnel links the Temple of Koricancha with the Convent of Santa Catalina or Marcahuasi,

Picture #37
Two more foundations for towers can be seen on the top of the Fortress of Sacsahuaman among the ancient Incan ruins.

THE CITY OF NEPHI 179

with the main Cathedral or Temple of Inca Wiracocha, with the Palace of Huascar, with the Temple of Manco Capac or Colcampata, and with the Huamanmarca. All of these buildings are in a perfect astronomical alignment, which confirms that ancient Peruvians also guided their constructions by the location of the Sun, the Moon, and the constellations. See the picture of the Avenue of the Sun (Avenida del Sol), #38 of Cusco. Ref 22.

Of course the motivation for such work is the search for the hidden Inca treasure that eluded the Spanish and Pizarro back in 1533. It has been traditionally thought that the Incas hid the bulk of their temple treasure in a deep nearby lake or possibly buried it in the secret tunnels under the city to keep it from falling into the hands of the European invaders. These tunnels under Cusco have been abandoned and condemned for centuries and were in disrepair even when the Spaniards arrived. Everyone who entered never returned and died, so the conquistadores sealed up the entrances for safety sake. Anselm Pi, President of Bohic Ruz Explorer has said:

> "We know that the accumulation of metals over a long period of time, in an enclosed and humid space, such as the subsoil of Cusco can create toxic substances such as cyanide, mercury or chloride. Inhaling these is probably what killed explorers in times past. But we enter prepared." Ref 22.

Whether or not the tunnels can be reconstructed and entered using special suits and breathing air is not as important as the artefacts to be recovered. It would be very important for instance if ancient records could be discovered which would not only prove that the ancient Pre-Inca peoples did have a writing system but also that could collaborate the Book of Mormon writings. King Mosiah I, probably, was able to take most of his records with him to Zarahemla, so to expect any ancient records of the original Nephites is a long shot. However, Limhi and his people left the City of Nephi in haste and the possibility of leftovers of records of his kingdom and era are a better possibility. Such records of course would be an invaluable find that could substantiate the entire work of Joseph Smith and the Restoration.

Picture #38 The main tunnel starts under the Avenue of the Sun from the Temple of Koricancha and its garden in the center of the photo to the main Cathedral in the Plaza de Armas in the lower left.

Astronomical Alignment of Incan Empire

There is great evidence that the Pre-Colombian cultures of the Andes studied verdantly the stars and their astronomical alignment in the universe. They organized their whole civilization on a forty-five degree axis west of due north. They built their cities based on this alignment with incredible accuracy. It is called today the 'Southern Cross'. It remains a great Incan religious symbol of heaven, earth, and the underworld. The following figures show how this brilliant culture applied these principles.

A combined map in the next figure shows the forty-five degree line of the major Incan cities all lined up in an astrological configuration that is part of the 'Southern Cross'.

Figures #28 & 29
Show the Andean or Incan Southern Cross.

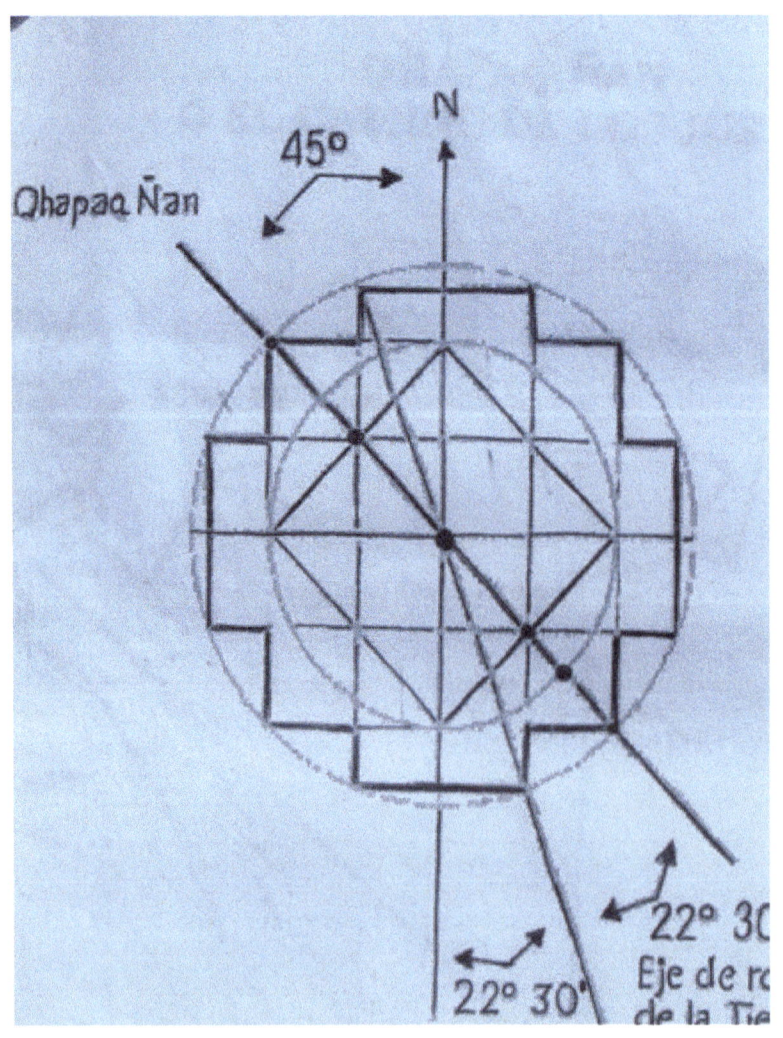

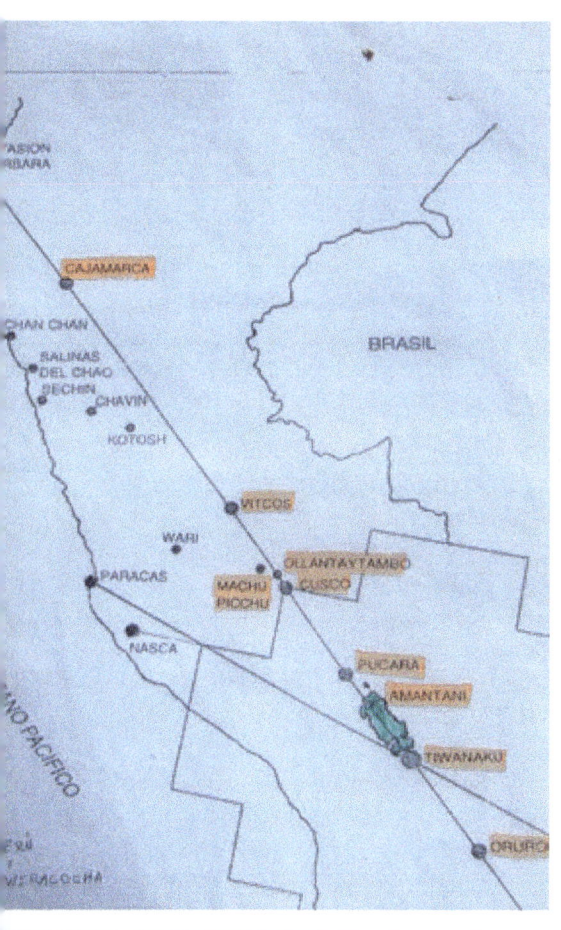 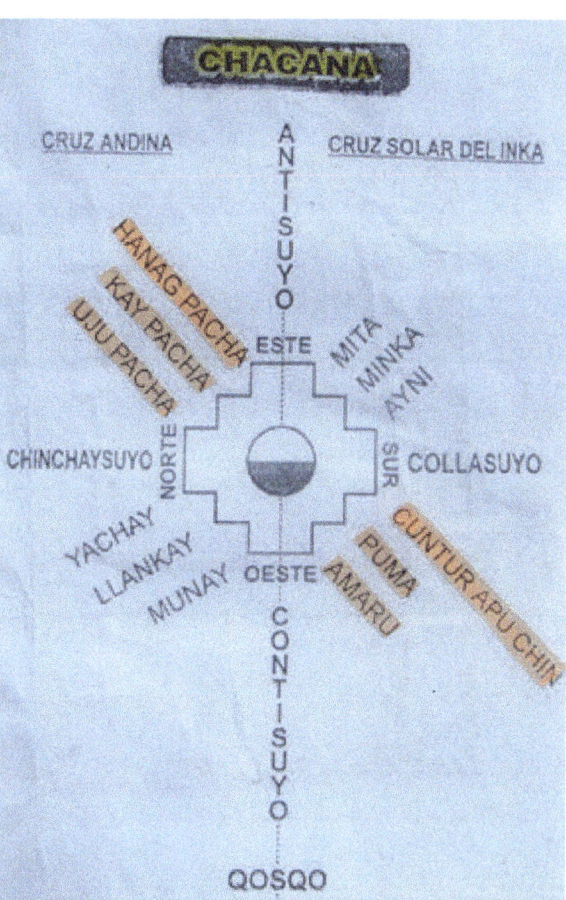

Figures 30 & 31 The first figure shows a map of the main Incan cities in a unique alignment. The second figure shows how that alignment corresponds to the 'Southern Cross' of Incan theology. It follows a straight line 45 degrees from true north.

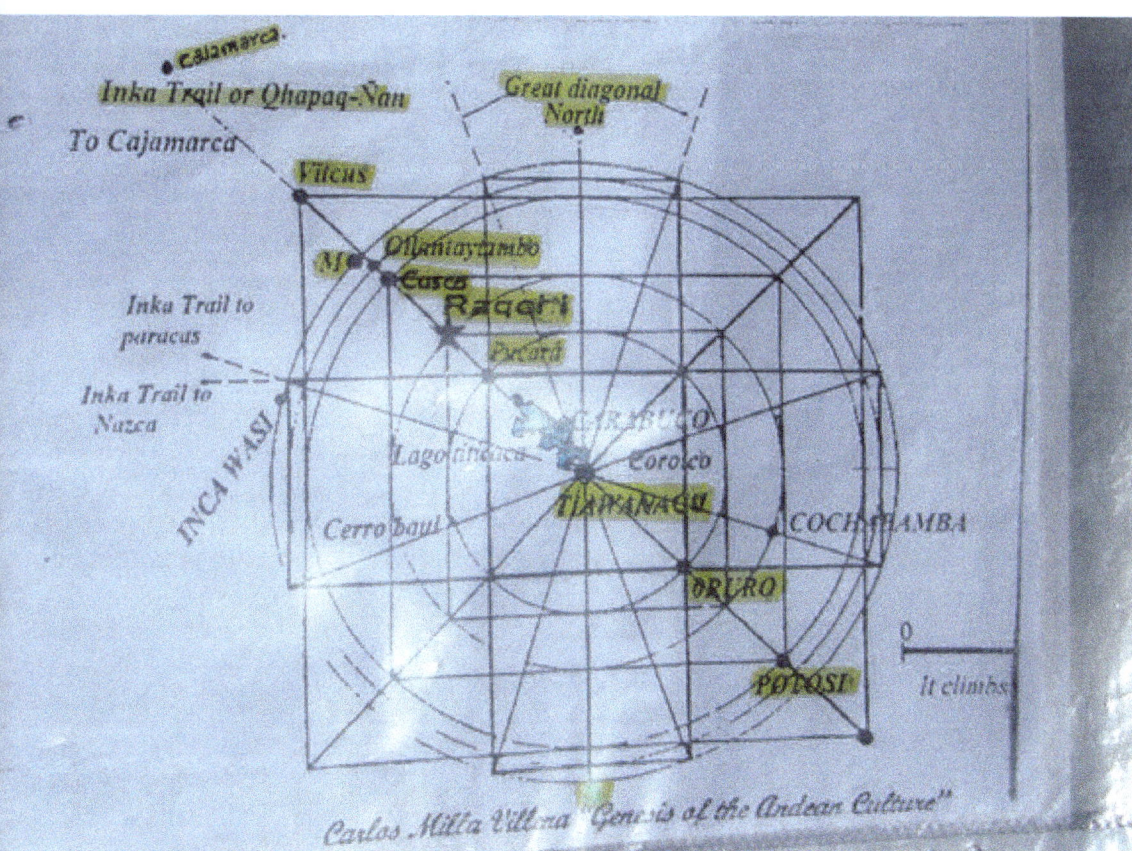

Figure 32 Combined Map of the Incan Empire on the Southern Cross symbol.

THE CITY OF NEPHI 183

Modern Cusco Today

This modern metropolis today is still the capitol of its Peruvian District. It has been continuously inhabited now for over twenty-six hundred years. Cusco is a city with buses and cars much like any Spanish colonial city in Peru. It boasts an international airport and it is an important Peruvian tourist destination that is world renown for its Incan Ruins. The city enjoys an eternal spring like weather condition year round. It is truly an enjoyable climate, and the scenery is magnificent with the Andean Mountains surrounding this high altitude valley nestled in the middle.

Tourism is one of the primary economic activities today of the several hundred thousand residents of the city. Visitors can view city tours of the famous Cathedrals, the Plaza de Armas, and the Arts District. The Temple of Koricancha is now open for tours on Avenida del Sol (Avenue of the Sun) with its accompanying museum and temple gardens. Of course Cusco is the starting place for tours of Sacsahuaman, Machu Pichu, Pisca, The Sacred Valley, Ollantaytambo, and the Inca Hiking Trail, as well as a hundred other interesting places. Machu Pichu has to one of the best-preserved and best-known of all the Incan ruins. The shear majesty of this city and its surroundings set it apart from any other sight in the world. Machu Pichu is truly one of man's best accomplishments and one of the most beautiful of the magnificent wonders of the world.

Picture #39
Modern City of Cusco, Peru at an elevation of 11,000 feet above sea level.

THE CITY OF NEPHI

Summary of the City of Cusco

As a person wanders the narrow cobblestone streets of Cusco you can still see the amazing Incan stone work that is the foundation and walls of many of the old buildings in the city center. The city has recently launched an aggressive excavation of several Incan sites in the city center that can be viewed by the public. These new excavations promise to bring new archaeological opportunities to the world and hopefully wonderful new discoveries from this ancient habitation. These digs will be a great addition to the already rich treasure of ancient artefacts and scientific knowledge of the Chavin and Incan cultures that have occupied this beautiful valley for more than twenty-six hundred years.

In tourist bazaars and handcraft markets the visitors can buy many native llama and alpaca woven articles of clothing and Incan handicrafts. The Cuscoans are a hard working and industrious people. They are basically a remote, mysterious people today, that have come to know the modern world. Yet, they can still be seen using their traditional ways and relying on the heritage that made them a great historical culture.

Picture #40
These are the world famous ruins of Machu Pichu near Cusco, Peru.

Picture #41 New Archaeological dig being done in Cusco at present time.

Picture #42 The foot plough can still be seen in use today as it was used in ancient times.

190 CITY OF CUSCO, PERU

The Peruvian women can still be seen walking the streets with their native clothing and hats that are peculiar to their particular family or community. Cusco is still the trading capitol where the farmers and rural people come daily to sell their wares and produce. Cusco is still very much an agrarian society. It is a delightful blend of old and new that will captivate any tourist.

Picture #43
A typical Peruvian woman with the Peruvian flower on her hat.

{Facing Picture of Ch #9} An inside wall of the Temple of Koricancha showing the superb stonework and craftsmanship of the ancient artisans of Peru.

CHAPTER 9

TEMPLE OF NEPHI

Book of Mormon References

From the Book of Mormon we know that the Nephites built at least three temples in the 'Promised Land', the Temple of Nephi, the Temple of Zarahemla, and the Temple of Bountiful. There most assuredly could have been others, but these are the ones that are mentioned in the scriptures. This book is mostly concerned with Nephi and the temple that he built. It was the most important feature of the city of Nephi and probably where he spent most of his time and the remainder of his life (45 years) building it and serving his people in the Temple of the Lord. Nephi related the following:

> 16. "And I, Nephi, did build a temple; and I did construct it after the manner of the temple of Solomon save it were not built of so many precious things; for they were not to be found upon the land, wherefore, it could not be built like unto Solomon's temple. But the manner of the construction was like unto the temple of Solomon; and the workmanship thereof was exceedingly fine." 2Nephi 5:16

Revelation for Nephi's Temple

Nephi was a prophet of God. Because of his standing before the Lord, he was granted the opportunity to build this temple. We know from the scriptures that the Lord inspires his prophets to build these sacred edifices, and then shows them a pattern of how it is to be done. Moses, David, and then Solomon had the patterns of the tabernacle and then the Temple on Mount Zion revealed to them by revelation. Joseph Smith, Brigham Young, and other modern day prophets have had similar experiences. These revelations were sacred experiences, and Nephi does not record anything of this experience or the pattern of construction or the ordinances of the temple. This does not seem strange to us because we understand the sacredness of the temple, and the ordinances and covenants associated with it. In actuality Nephi could have written all these things down and recorded them on his plates in the portion that was sealed when Joseph Smith received them. What we do know is that he built a temple to the Lord, and that he did know about these things and undoubtedly passed them on to Jacob and Joseph and others. Centuries later there were temples in Zarahemla and also even in Bountiful where the Savior appeared to the Nephites, suggesting that these truths were passed down and other prophets also given instruction about temple rites and purposes. Obviously, the purpose of this temple like the others was to provide a holy place where the Lord could come and dwell among his covenant people. Here Nephi would have received knowledge, priesthood powers, officiated in the holy ordinances and performed the sacred rites necessary for the salvation of his people. It is very comforting to know that as prophet he would have spent more time here both in building the temple and serving in it, than anything else he did, and he only writes one verse regarding it, thus conserving the sacredness of the Temple for discussion only within its walls. It would have been the center of his world, the Navel of the Universe for this prophet of God. This edifice, the Temple of Koricancha, twenty-six hundred years later is still the most sacred and revered building in all of South America by the native people.

Temple of Solomon

Since Nephi says that he built the temple 'after the manner' of the Temple of Solomon, we should look at Solomon's Temple and see what exactly this reference means to us. King David spent a lifetime amassing materials to build the Temple of God such as: gold, silver, iron, and bronze, stone, and timbers of cedar. The temple took a good seven years to complete using a very large workforce, (200,000 laborers). The dimensions of Solomon's Temple were 45 feet high, 105 feet long, and 30 feet wide. The measurements of the Holy Place and the Holy of Holies were exactly twice those of Moses' Tabernacle. (See 1Kings 6:38)

Temple Symbolism

There are many interesting symbolisms that relate to the construction site of the Temple on Mount Zion. This sacred site was where Abraham offered up Isaac at the top of Mount Moriah. It served as a threshing floor for the Israelites to willow their wheat. The altar where David offered up his

Picture #44
The walls of the Temple of Koricancha have been so finely worked that they look like poured blocks of cement. Beautifully carved Andesite stone worked to perfection make this the finest example of stone masonry in all of South America.

196 TEMPLE OF NEPHI

sacrifices was located there. The gate of the temple would face east to point to the coming of Christ.

"The temple was located on the top of the mountain. Because the sanctuary was located halfway between heaven and earth, it served as an ideal meeting place for God and man." The temple was built on the North side of the mountain because God was thought to have resided near the North Star. (*The Gate of Heaven* by Matthew B. Brown p.111-112)

Therefore several attributes of Solomon's temple would also most assuredly be physical characteristics of Nephi's temple, as well. First of all, the temple would be the focal point, or jewel of the city of Nephi which was the 'Center of the Universe, the Navel of the World'. Second it would be located at the top of the mountain valley. Third it would be also at the north end of the valley, half way between heaven and earth. Fourth, the temple gate or entrance would need to also face east. Most temples built throughout history and even in modern times are quite different in size, functionality, and design, but they also have many similarities. We assume that since Nephi comments that the temple he built was after the 'manner of the Temple of Solomon' that he used it as a model for his temple. However, this does not mean that Nephi's temple would be an exact replica in size, design, or function. It means in a very real sense that the manner of construction was like the Temple of Solomon namely exquisitely carved stone work. We do know that Nephi was very young when he would have seen the temple in Jerusalem, and he would never have functioned in the temple itself or knew about it entirely at such a young age as to be able to copy it. So, we propose that most of the knowledge of his design and function of the temple came to him directly from God through revelation.

Picture #45 The temple block was the center of the city. The main streets of the city bisected the temple square and divided the city and the empire into four quadrants. The Cathedral of Santa Domingo atop the ancient Temple of Koricancha, conforms to all the criteria.

THE CITY OF NEPHI 197

Navel of the Earth

The temple area of Mount Moriah also served as a threshing floor symbolizing the bringing in of the sheaves to the central area where the wheat could be separated from the chaff. It is a time honored symbol of separating the wheat from the chaff, the good from the bad, or the worthy from the unclean, the Children of God from the Children of Men. The temple has a way of doing that very well.

> "One authority on symbolism states that the threshing floor is an *omphalos*, or navel symbol, because the hemispherical hub of grain, which the oxen tread a circular path around, resembles the point at which the navel cord is bound. And indeed, the temple on Mount Zion was looked upon by the Hebrew people as the sacred center or navel of the earth." (*The Gate of Heaven* by Matthew B. Brown p.113) Ref 20.

The navel is also a symbol of our need to receive constant nourishment from our parent. This nourishment is a spiritual need to communicate with our Heavenly Father through the umbilical cord of prayer and personal revelation.

> "The sacred space of the Jerusalem temple is set apart from all other spaces of the earth, not only because Yahweh has chosen Zion as his...'resting place', but also because... the site of Zion was related to the navel of the earth. Solomon's temple is built on a rock which is the earth-center, the world mountain, the foundation stone of creation, the extremity of the umbilical cord which provides a link between heaven, earth, and the underworld." (Samuel Terrien, *The Omphalos Myth and Hebrew Religion*, Vetus Testamentum, vol. 20, no. 3, July 1970, 317). Ref 21.

In the apocryphal book of *Jubilees* (8:19), we read that Mount Zion is the center of the navel of the earth.

Manner of Construction

Nephi says that the 'Manner of Construction' of his temple was like unto the Temple of Solomon. What does that mean exactly? The Temple of Solomon was rebuilt twice and only parts of the original construction remain, which would be the foundation stones of the temple mount or outer wall of the temple courtyard. The original foundation stones of the temple's courtyard walls can still be seen today. The final Jerusalem temple of course was destroyed in 70 A.D. by the Romans. One of the most incredible tours of Jerusalem that can be taken today is a walk through the Tunnel of the West Wall which starts by the Western Wailing Wall of the temple block. This modern tunnel was hewn out to expose the rest of the Western Wall, and follows the course underground of the foundation of the temple mount and courtyard wall, some 23 feet below the street level of the present day.

The huge blocks of stone that form the foundation are colossal and monstrous in size and weight with some probably weighing upwards of 100-200 tons. These stones fit so perfectly on top of each other that cement was not needed to bond them together and a knife blade cannot be put between their joints. Truly remarkable were these craftsman that were responsible for such construction without the modern tools and equipment that we have today. Such construction can only be seen today in a few places, notably they include: the foundations of the great pyramids of Egypt, the temple mount at Jerusalem and in the construction of the ancient Pre-Inca buildings in Peru (particularly the Temple of Koricancha).

The exact description of the stone masonry of Solomon's Temple we do not have, however, a very good description of the construction process is found in the scriptures in 2 Chronicles where it states:

> "1. And Solomon determined to build an house for the name of the Lord, and an house for his kingdom.
>
> 2. And Solomon told out threescore and ten thousand men to bear burdens, and fourscore thousand to hew (quarry stone) in the mountain, and three thousand and six hundred to oversee them," 2 Chronicles 2:1-2

Therefore, the process of building the temple took seven years with 80,000 stone masons hewing the stone in the quarries necessary for all of the courses in the temple walls and courtyard walls. If the temple stones averaged two feet in height as an example then twenty-five courses of stone would have been needed to complete the walls to a height of 45 feet, which were covered with a roof made of cedar trees from Lebanon. The stones would have been shaped and dressed at the quarry perfectly so that no chiseling needed to be done at the sacred temple site. The stones would be larger on the bottom tiers graduating to smaller stones as the walls rose in height. They would be perfectly hewn and shaped so that no mortar was needed to bond the stones together. The wall would have a 'leaning or Eygptian style' construction that was common in this time period. 70,000 workers were required to transport the finished blocks to the temple mount as well as other building materials during the seven year construction period.

Nephi of course was a young boy when he left Jerusalem. He had not been involved in major construction projects of this magnitude. Neither had he worked as a skilled craftsman in stonework or other building trades. The other brothers and Zoram were not accomplished in these areas either. Nephi no doubt had seen these great buildings and knew of the 'manner

Picture #46
Walls of the Temple of Koricancha are larger at base and have a 'leaning look' making the construction style very Egyptian.

of their construction' but this would have been a feat for even a seasoned and skilled workforce let alone a group of adventurers and wanderers. He necessarily needed the help of the Lord to accomplish the construction of a temple after 'the manner of the Temple of Solomon'.

The manner of construction of the Temple of Nephi was necessarily done using the local Andesite Granite stone similar to the famed Jerusalem Stone. The beautiful crafted fine stone work was what set the two temples apart from all other buildings along with the finished height of the temples. These artisans were talented stone masons that were required to shape the stones off site so that the sound of the chisel and mallet would not be heard at the sacred temple mount. The monolithic base stones for the temple walls were one to two hundred tons in weight and were an incredible challenge to transport from the quarries to the temple grounds. The temple blocks were colossal stones magnificently dressed by master craftsmen that would make their work celebrated for generations. These stones were set a top one another so finely carved and fit together that no mortar was needed to bond the blocks together. The stones were larger at the base and smaller as the wall courses rose in height. The Temple of Nephi can be described as being constructed in an Egyptian-like 'leaning' manner. There could not be a more precise language than what Nephi used when he compared the two temples, that their 'manner of construction' was the same. The finished work prompted Nephi to say, "....**But the manner of the construction was like unto the temple of Solomon; and the workmanship thereof was exceedingly fine.**"

Temple during the Time of Limhi

When Zeniff returned again to the Land of Nephi then he records that his people repaired the walls of the city and the buildings:

> 8. "And we began to build buildings, and to repair the walls of the city, yea, even the walls of the city of Lehi-Nephi, and the city of Shilom." Mosiah 9:8

During the reign of the wicked King Noah, Zeniff's son, the temple was modified, and many other beautiful buildings were also built using the burdensome taxes of the people. He also built a very high tower presumably as a look out tower for danger. The record of the Book of Mormon states:

> 8. "And it came to pass that king Noah built many elegant and spacious buildings; and he ornamented them with fine work

of wood, and of all manner of precious things, of gold, and of silver, and of iron, and of brass, and of ziff, and of copper;

9. And he also built him a spacious palace, and a throne in the midst thereof, all of which was of fine wood and was ornamented with gold and silver and with precious things.

10. And he also caused that his workmen should work all manner of fine work within the walls of the **temple**, of fine wood, and of copper, and of brass.

12. And it came to pass that he built a **tower near the temple**; yea, a very high tower, even so high that he could stand upon the top thereof and overlook the land of Shilom, and also the land of Shemlon, which was possessed by the Lamanites; and he could even look over all the land round about.

13. And it came to pass that he caused many buildings to be built in the land Shilom; and he caused a great tower to be built on the hill north of the land of Shilom; which had been a resort for the children of the land; and thus he did do with the riches which he obtained by the taxation of his people." Mosiah 11:8-10 & 12-13

These verses clearly state that the temple was in use and worked on and maintained during the time of Zeniff and his son, Noah, and his grandson, Limhi. Also, of interest are the 'very high towers' that were built during this time by the temple and at the resort or fortress of Shilom. Another reference to the temple can be found during the time of Limhi when Ammon came up from the city of Zarahemla to find the people of Zeniff. The Book of Mormon relates:

17. "And now, it came to pass on the morrow that king Limhi sent a proclamation among all his people, that thereby they might gather themselves together to the **temple**, to hear the words which he should speak unto them." Mosiah 7:17

At the time the temple was a central gathering place where the people would come for instruction and to muster. Probably one of the most beloved characters of the Book of Mormon was Gideon, servant of King Limhi. He presented a plan to Limhi about how they could escape from the

Land of Nephi and the Lamanites so that they could return to Zarahemla. This is a key feature of the temple and the city of Nephi for archaeologists and Book of Mormon students today. Gideon said:

> 6. "Behold the back pass, through the back wall, on the back side of the city. The Lamanites, or the guards of the Lamanites, by night are drunken; therefore let us send a proclamation among all this people that they gather together their flocks and herds, that they may drive them into the wilderness by night.
>
> 7. And I will go according to thy command and pay the last tribute of wine to the Lamanites, and they will be drunken; and we will pass through the secret pass on the left of their camp when they are drunken and asleep." Mosiah 22:6-7

Could Gideon have referred to a secret passage way or tunnel that started at the temple and went underground up to the resort north of the city of Nephi to Shilom and to the fortress. With the Lamanites living in the land of Shemlon to the left of Shilom as they traveled north they could have moved thousands of people through the secret passage way undetected until they reached the tower at the northern part of Shilom and into the wilderness. The flocks and herds of course were driven to wilderness areas to the north ahead of time to normal grazing areas in preparation for the exodus. In the cover of darkness and with the Lamanites in a drunken state they made good their departure from the land of Nephi and bondage from the Lamanites.

After Limhi and his group of Nephites leave the city and the temple area, the Temple of Nephi is never mentioned again in the Book of Mormon. We assume it still existed and was used down through the centuries. The temple obviously was one of the best built and nicest buildings in the city, if not the best. But its use and purposes could have changed and probably did change dramatically during the following centuries of Lamanite occupation.

The Temple of Nephi was a gathering place and a mustering place in the City of Nephi, the center of the earth, the navel of the universe for the Nephite people. It would have been the center of knowledge and spiritual growth. One can only imagine the importance of this sacred building and its surrounding gardens that was established in their Nephite culture for 450 years.

The Temple of Nephi after the Time of Limhi

The Lamanites who later occupied the city and controlled the temple would have also known of its special nature and its importance. They would have most likely revered it, been wary of its spiritual significance, and also most likely superstitious of the temple and the religion of their enemies. The temple is never mentioned during the centuries of Lamanite control of the Land of Nephi. However, many times during the history of these people, the Lamanites were led by dissident or apostate Nephites who would have definitely been aware of the temple and the religion of the Nephites. Even if they did not practice Christianity or the religion of the Nephites they would have taught the other Lamanites about the importance of the temple. Also, at many times during their history, the Lamanites were converted to Christianity and became a righteous people.

As well, many times there were visiting Nephite missionaries who also would have known about the importance of the temple and the temple rites. It would have been hard to believe that Ammon and his brethren

Figure #33 Artist's rendition of the Temple of Koricancha

would not have used the temple during their fourteen year mission among the Lamanites in the Land of Nephi. In fact in Alma it mentions that these sons of Mosiah were given free access to their temples and even taught the people at the temples (Alma 23:2 and 26:29). Even to the wicked portion of the Lamanites, the City of Nephi became their capitol and the center of their world, their "Chief City". As late as 29 B.C. Nephi and Lehi, sons of Helaman II went to the Land of Nephi to preach to the Lamanites and with power and authority and with many mighty miracles from God they converted most of the Lamanite Nation.

> Hel 5:50. "....that the more part of the Lamanites were convinced of them, because of the greatness of the evidences which they had received.

> Hel 6:1. ....the Lamanites had become, the more part of them, a righteous people, insomuch that their righteousness did exceed that of the Nephites, because of their firmness and their steadiness in the faith." Helaman 5:50, and 6:1

SUMMARY OF THE TEMPLE OF NEPHI

To summarize the important characteristics of the Temple of Nephi, we discover the following attributes:

1. The Temple of Nephi was built after the manner of the Temple of Solomon in method of construction. The design and function was similar, but not necessarily exactly the same. The physical location of the temple would be on the north side of the top of the valley, with the temple facing east are some of the similarities.
2. The manner of construction of the Temple of Nephi was physically similar to the Temple of Solomon except for the precious stones and other precious things of Solomon's Temple. This would include colossal and exquisite stone work.
3. The temple block had a history of being a sacred edifice for centuries of the different cultures that occupied the city. It was their center of civilization, or chief city, the navel or center of their universe.
4. We know that Nephi's temple also had a garden associated with it. These gardens probably would have had fountains and renowned beauty.

5. The temple was associated with a very tall tower that could overlook the surrounding cities of Shemlon and Shilom.
6. The temple had secret passage ways or tunnels connecting it to other areas to the north.
7. The Temple of Nephi was a sacred edifice that was revered for many centuries during the occupation of different groups of people after the original Nephite culture.
8. During the Zeniff-Noah-Limhi era the temple was refurbished and aggrandized. Presumably, it was given extra gold and silver ornamentation over and above the original temple construction.

It should also be noted that the City of Nephi is never mentioned in the great destruction when the 'Land was Changed' at the time of the coming of Christ. Also, of course the temple is never mentioned after the time of Christ either. So, it is likely a good possibility that the city survived and prospered after the great destructions. That is only speculation, but it would make sense that a major city and inhabited land like the City of Nephi would have been part of the list of cities mentioned in Third Nephi as having been destroyed if it had suffered such a fate. So, correspondingly, we should also assume that the Temple of Nephi also survived the great destruction if the City of Nephi survived.

{Facing Picture Ch #10} A museum model of the Temple of Koricancha when first seen by the conquistadors when they arrived in Cusco in 1533.

CHAPTER 10

TEMPLE OF KORICANCHA

Pre-Columbian Temple

First, we will take another look from the perspective of the Spanish Chroniclers and others of what the Temple of Koricancha or the Temple of the Sun was like before Pizarro and the Spanish conquistadors came to Peru. Hernando de Soto and other early conquistadors were awe-struck the first time that they saw the temple in the late afternoon with the sun gleaming off from the golden temple. It was obviously quite impressive to the Spanish, and they quickly went to work dismantling more than 700 panels of pure gold from off the exterior and interior walls of the temple. Some of these panels were ¼ to ½ inches thick and 2 feet by 4 feet weighing between 10 and 25 lbs. The panels, like all the beautiful golden temple artefacts, were melted down into ingots for shipment to Spain and distribution to the conquering army. On the beautiful stone walls of the temple can still be seen today the marks or places of attachment for the golden panels.

Picture #47
The Golden Temple of Koricancha as it appeared before Pizarro's arrival.

Garcilaso de la Vega in his book, *The Incas* described the Temple of Koricancha as follows:

"All the Incas enriched this city and, among its countless monuments, the Temple of the Sun remained the principal object of their attention. They vied with one another in ornamenting it with incredible wealth, each Inca seeking to surpass his predecessor. Indeed, the splendors of this temple were such that I should not venture to describe them, had not all Spanish historians of Peru done the same. But nothing that they have written, nor anything that I might add, could ever depict it as it really was." Ref 3 p.75

It appears that throughout the centuries the various cultures and ruling civilizations all had a hand in enriching the Temple of Koricancha. It was a sacred place for all and a depository of their spoils and precious treasures. Gracilaso goes on to say:

> "The Temple of the Sun was located on the site that today is occupied by the Church of San Dominique, and its walls, which are made of highly polished stone, still exist. What we shall call the high altar, although this expression did not exist among the Indians, was to the east, and the roof, which was very high, was of wood, covered with straw. The four walls were hung with plaques of gold, from top to bottom, and a likeness of the Sun topped the high altar. This likeness was made of a gold plaque twice as thick as those that paneled the walls, and was composed of a round face, prolonged by rays and flames, the way the Spanish painters represent it; the whole thing was so immense that it occupied the entire back of the temple, from one wall to the other. There was no other idol in this temple, nor in any other, for the Sun was the only god of the Incas, whatever people may say on this subject. When the Spaniards entered Cuzco, this likeness of the Sun, as the result of a division of property, fell into the hands of one of the early conquistadors......"

> "On either side of this Sun, were kept the numerous mummies of former Inca kings, which were so well preserved that they seemed to be alive. They were seated on their golden thrones resting on plaques of the same metal, and they looked directly at the visitor.....The main door of the temple opened to the north, as it does today, and there were several others, of less importance, which were used for services in the temple. All of these doors were covered with plaques of gold and the walls of the building were crowned on the outside with a gold band, three feet wide, that went all around it."

> "The temple was prolonged by a square cloister with an adjoining wall and crowned by a gold band like the one we have just described. The Spaniards replaced this by a plaster band of the same width that could be seen on the walls, which were still standing, when I left Peru. The three other sides of the cloister gave on to five square rooms, that had no communication between them, and were roofed over in the form of a pyramid."

> "The first of these rooms was dedicated to the Moon, the bride of the Sun, and for this reason it was nearest to the main building. It was entirely paneled with silver, and a likeness of the Moon, with the face of a woman, decorated it in the same way that the Sun decorated the larger building. The Indians offered no sacrifices to her, but they came to visit her and begged her intercession, as to the sister-bride of the Sun and to the mother of all the Incas. They called her Mamaquilla, which means our mother the Moon. The bodies of queens were laid away in this Temple, just as those of the kings were kept in the other. Mama Occlo, the mother of Huaina

Capac, occupied the place of honor, before the likeness of the Moon, because she had given birth to such a son."

"The room nearest that of the Moon was devoted to Venus, to the Pleiades and to all the stars. As we said before, Venus was honored as the Sun's page, who accompanies him on his way, now following him, now preceding him. The Indians considered the other stars as servants of the Moon, and this was why they were represented near her. The constellation of the Pleiades was particularly revered because of the regularity and perfection of its well-grouped design."

"This room was hung with silver, like that of the Moon, and the ceiling was dotted with stars, like the firmament. The next room was dedicated to lightning, and to thunder, which were both expressed by the single name, *illapa*. If they said: 'Did you hear *illapa*?' it was understood as "thunder." And if they said: 'Did you see *illapa*?' or '*illapa* struck there,' this meant "lightning."

"Both were respected as servants of the Sun, just as the gentiles used to consider lightning as Jupiter's own weapon. This room was entirely covered with gold, but neither lightning nor thunder were represented there, because they would not have known how to go about it."

"The fourth room was devoted to the rainbow, which they said had descended from the Sun, and which figured on the scutcheon of the Inca kings. It was entirely covered with gold and the rainbow was painted, in beautiful colors, across the entire surface of one of the walls. They called the rainbow *cuichu* and revered it very specially. When it appeared, they immediately put their hands over their mouths through fear, they said, that it might make their teeth decay. I can't say why."

"The fifth and last room was reserved for the high priest and his assistants, who were all of royal blood. They did not live there but met there in council, either to give hearings, or to decide upon the sacrifices and all that had to be done in connection with the service of the temple. This parlor was paneled with gold, in the same way as the others." Ref 3, p. 75-77.

Location of the Temple of Koricancha

Cusco is divided archeologically into two city areas Hanan-Cuzco and Huron-Cuzco. The lower city, Huron-Cuzco is the oldest part of the city, or our City of Nephi. The temple of Koricancha or our Temple of Nephi is located in the northern most part of the highest area of the old city. In the days of the conquistadors the temple had a very high tower associated with it. The tower and its foundation is now completely gone. The Cusco valley is a long and wide valley that increases in elevation to about 11,000

feet as it ascends to the north with mountains encircling around it. The Temple of Koricancha is located exactly as the requirements with the Temple of Solomon. It is actually the navel of the Puma in the ancient layout of the city. It is situated in the highest place of the most northern area of the old part of the city, literally at the tops of the mountains. The newer city of Hanan-Cuzco, or Shilom of the Book of Mormon is centered ten blocks further north at the crest of the valley. This newer part of the city of Cusco was built later by the wicked King Noah when he constructed many beautiful and spacious buildings. Today, the Plaza de Armas or main city square is the center of Cusco city where the Main Cathedral, and other important government buildings are located as well. This Hanan-Cusco or

Picture #48
Two rooms of the Temple of Koricancha

Picture #49
Front steps of the modern day Santo Domingo Chapel.

Shilom contained at the extreme northern end the resort or fortress of the modern day Sacsahuaman with its three towers.

Importance of the Temple of Koricancha

Today, the local native inhabitants of Cusco have a unique feeling about the ancient Temple of Koricancha. It has not been forgotten by the faithful Peruvians even though for nearly four centuries a Catholic Cathedral has been built over the top of their precious temple. They revere this sacred temple as the center of their Inca religion and the most important and sacred place in not just Cusco but in all of Peru and South America.

Today many modern native groups do not like the fact that the Catholic Church has control and ownership of the Temple of Koricancha and are trying to influence the political powers to give this priceless legacy back to the native people. Below are comments from one such group:

>"Raymundo Bejar Navarro, an archaeologist, climbs the adobe wall up onto the grounds of the Santo Domingo monastery here in the center of town. Shaking his head, he complains that the four resident monks are refusing to let his scientific team dig in the area. Defiantly, looking up at the towering, 350-year-old Spanish church, he hisses through his teeth, 'They should tear this down.' The reason for such emotion is that the Santo Domingo church and monastery sit

Picture #50
Another view from the north side of the Temple of Koricancha with Santo Domingo Chapel built on top.

atop the holiest shrine of the Inca culture – the Temple of the Sun, or Koricancha in Quechua. And Mr. Bejar is leading a three-year effort to restore the temple…..Until conquered by the Spanish, the Temple of the Sun was the center of the vast Inca empire that stretched from northern Venezuela to Patagonia in southern Argentina. Here was the repository of the realm's gold treasure, showcase of its exquisite stone carving technology and central seat of government. As was customary when the Spaniards conquered an area, they imposed Catholicism on the Incas and used the Koricancha structure as a church. In 1650 an earthquake destroyed part of the Dominican Church, so the Spanish tore most of the temple down and used the finely cut stones to build the existing church and monastery. In 1953 another quake hit the building. Many of the Spanish-built walls collapsed, revealing parts of the original structure hidden for centuries. In reconstructing Santo Domingo, church officials agreed not to build on some of the existing Inca walls. For Jesus Cheque, a Quechua Indian working on the digging project, the idea of the Santo Domingo church resting atop the Inca temple is a bitter one, and he says flatly that he wants the church torn down. 'It's the symbol of the oppression of our culture, the abuse of my Andean past,' he said. 'Where is my place to worship? They have stolen the stones of my temple.'" Ref 14. *The Incas – Empire of Blood and Gold* p. 156.

Sacred Ground

The Temple of God has always been considered as Sacred or Holy Ground. We have complete reverence and respect for these hallowed places in all the world. The first known reference to the tradition of removing your shoes before entering such a place was when Moses communicated with God on Mount Sinai. The account goes as follows:

> 4. "And when the Lord saw that he turned aside to see, God called unto him out of the midst of the bush, and said, Moses, Moses. And he said, Here am I.
> 5. And he said, Draw not nigh hither: put off thy shoes from off thy feet, for the place whereon thou standest is holy ground." Exodus 3:4-5

In like manner it was unlawful to go into the Temple of Koricancha or approach its sacred ground without having removed your shoes. It is probably not a coincidence that this phenomena of 'removing your shoes' to approach the temple is unique. It is the only known place in South

America with a similar tradition. The chronicler, Garcilaso de la Vega says of the temple:

> "It was forbidden to enter the grand area, or the temple itself, without first having removed one's shoes…..Mention should also be made of a cross street, running east and west, that cut across the four roads to the temple at one particular point, beyond which it was forbidden to continue with one's shoes on. From this point to the entrance of the temple properly speaking, there remained about two hundred steps to be taken." Ref 3. p. 79.

Picture #51
The Temple of Koricancha has an interior courtyard where the Altar of Santa Rosa is located and it is the possible location for one of the entrances to the secret tunnels. The courtyard had a fountain or wash basin originally located with the sacred alter for sacrifices.

Temple Workers

Who worked in the temple during the Inca Dynasty, or was the temple just used as a museum for the mummified remains of the Inca kings? It appears that according to ancient Inca tradition the temple was presided over by a 'High Priest' who received revelation in the temple and officiated in the temple performing specified temple rites. Garcilaso again makes some interesting comments concerning the temple priests:

> "The name of the high priest was *uilac-umu*, which the Spaniards have made into *vilaoma*. This name means 'he who speaks of divine matters,' from the verb *uilla*, to speak and *umu*, the divine. It was he who communicated to the people the decisions of the supreme god, the Sun, as well as his own interpretations of dreams and all the signs in which he believed he could read the divine will."

> "In my youth, I recall having seen three of these five rooms, still almost intact, all that was missing being the silver and gold paneling. Nothing remained, however, of the two others, those of the Moon and the stars. Outside these rooms, four recesses had been hollowed out in the thickness of the walls, on each of the three sides of the cloister that they enclosed. These recesses were covered with carving on their entire surface and lined with gold plaques incrusted with emeralds and turquoises, that espoused the relief of the sculptures. During the Sun festivals the Inca sat in one of them, on one or the other side of the cloister, according to the feast day being celebrated."

> "The twelve doors of the sacred rooms that opened on to the cloister were paneled in gold, with the exception of those of the Moon and the stars, which were in silver."

> "There were many more, smaller rooms in the enclosure of the Sun temple, which were used to lodge the priests and servants of these sacred precincts. All of these men were chosen from among the Incas, some of royal blood, others merely privileged, and access to these premises was forbidden to men who were not of Inca blood, and to all women, without consideration of rank or birth: even the wives and daughters of the king were denied entrance here. The priests succeeded one another in the service of the temple, according to the quarters of the Moon. During that time they could have nothing to do with their wives, nor could they even leave the temple, by day or by night."

> "The servants of the temple, such as porters, cleaners, cooks, cup bearers, lackeys, jewellers, weavers, or others, were chosen from the same villages as were those in the service of the King, and these posts were considered to be obligatory responsibilities incumbent upon the villages in question. For the service of these two houses, that of the king

and that of the Sun, were equal in all things, like that of father and son, with this single difference, that no sacrifices were offered in the king's house, and there were no women among the servants of the Sun. In everything else, the two houses were equal in grandeur and in majesty."

"Sacrifices were offered up in different spots, that varied according to their importance and solemnity. The grand area of the temple, however, was reserved for the richest of them all, called Raimi, which took place during the principal Sun festival. Sacrifices were also offered up on the parvis, on the occasion of other festivals to which the provinces and different nations of the empire sent delegations to bear offerings and dance in the capitol." Ref 3. p. 78-79.

Picture #52
Santo Domingo was built over the top of the Temple of Koricancha. Here is a picture of the Cathedral pillars that used the Temple as a foundation for its walls and roof structure. The Temple of Koricancha was virtually earthquake proof.

220 TEMPLE OF KORICANCHA

The Church of Santo Domingo

In 1560 the Catholic Priests of the Dominican Order were given the Temple of Koricancha by Hernando Pizarro, Francisco Pizarro's brother, who received it in 1536 in the first dispersal of lands and buildings to the Spanish conquistadors. The priests built a church and monastery over the sacred temple using the smaller stones from the temple and temple walls to build their own church. The church was destroyed twice by earthquakes, once in 1650 and then again in 1953. Each time the church was rebuilt the Cathedral was destroyed, but the walls of the Temple remained perfectly intact and without any damage from the earthquakes. When it was rebuilt in 1953, the Catholic Church promised to preserve the remaining walls and give some public access to the ancient Incan temple.

"The church is indeed a mixture of the two conflicting cultures. Its foundations and supporting walls are of the exquisitely carved Inca stones, made out of andesite, that were carved with stone tools from quarries miles away, and so finely shaped at the building site that no mortar was needed. Even today, a knife does not fit between the joints. Above the Inca masonry is the Spanish construction of roughly cut stones put together with adobe mortar, giving the church a two-tone texture. Inside, large parts of the gilded baroque monastery have been removed to reveal four stone chambers of the original Inca temple. Recently the digging has produced a new phase of the centuries-old struggle between the conquerors and conquered

Picture #53
The beautiful Temple of Koricancha is one of the famous tourist spots in Cusco. It is a wonderful photo opportunity with the Temple Gardens in the foreground with the young Peruvian girls.

THE CITY OF NEPHI

of Peru, between the modern-day Roman Catholic Church and the descendants of the Incas, who yielded to Francisco Pizarro in 1532. 'They have so many churches throughout Peru,' Mr. Bejar said. 'Why do they have to have one right on top of the holiest Inca site: I thought this was the year when the church was apologizing for past abuses, If they abused anyone, they abused the Incas.' Mr. Bejar, who is a Roman Catholic, has beliefs that have not sat well with the church hierarchy. 'The capricious Mr. Bejar is pretending to take down a church that has been declared a world monument by Unesco,' said the Revd. Domingo Gamarra, director of the monastery. 'The church represents the meeting of two cultures. What he is doing is anti-Christian, and we will defend the church to the very end.'" Ref 14.

Koricancha as a Tourist Center

In 1991 the mayor of Cusco, Mr. Daniel Estrada, tried to resurrect their besieged tourist industry which had been hurt by outbreaks of cholera and problems with guerrilla violence. He made a very important decision to bolster the sagging tourist industry in his city, that centered around the Inca ruins of Cusco and the breathtaking ruins of Machu Picchu.

"'This is a victimized society, oppressed and suppressed for centuries, and we intend to change that by being sensitive to the Andean beliefs,' Mr. Estrada said. 'For them Cuzco is the Sacred City.'....But Koricancha represents his most ambitious project. Using $2 million of the municipality's funds, the Mayor bought the land around the temple, tore down the existing houses and began excavating in the area that once was the outer court....A restored Koricancha is considered to be a major piece in reviving tourism in Cuzco. But if the dispute is not resolved, it may look like just nondescript ruins next to a colonial church. And, what's more, the most scientifically important site of Koricancha – the central temple chamber – may never be touched by archaeologists, since it rests directly under the church's sanctuary. 'The monks don't want to let anyone dig, because they are afraid they'll lose the property.' Said Prof. John Rowe, an archaeologist at the University of California in Berkeley and an adviser to the Koricancha project. 'They are only a few monks in a huge piece of property, but no one here wants to take on the church.'" Ref 15. Nash, Nathaniel C. New York Times 1993.

Manner of Construction

The Temple of Koricancha is very unique in its 'manner of construction' compared to the other Pre-Inca buildings in Cusco from its time period. First of all the hard Andesite Stone blocks that are used in the construction of the temple have been dressed to such a fine degree that they fit perfectly one on top of another, almost like they were machine manufactured or poured from some ancient concrete mold.

The fine dressing of these temple stones is exquisite compared to other Incan buildings of the same time period. The stones are large at the bottom or foundation courses and weigh maybe a thousand pounds at most and grow progressively smaller to a few hundred pounds as the wall courses go

Picture #54
Inside the Temple of Koricancha

Picture #55 Temple walls were made with larger stones at the base and grew smaller as the wall courses went up causing the characteristic 'leaning or Egyptian' style construction. Notice also the intricate doorways and large mantle stones over the doorways which were also unique to Egyptian construction.

up in height. The finely cut nature of these stone walls are what defines the beauty of this building and the 'manner of construction' of the temple. More time and care was taken in its construction than any other building in Peru. The construction is said to be of 'Egyptian style' which means that the walls are thicker at the base, between 30-36 inches to 28-24 inches at the top, giving the wall a sense of 'leaning' which adds strength and stability to the structure. This manner of construction has allowed the temple walls to withstand the region's earthquakes down through the centuries. So, let us analyze this structure to see how uniquely it fits the required 'manner of construction' that Nephi says was similar to the temple of Solomon. First the temple was built of finely dressed stones of Cyclopean size. These stones are so beautifully carved that the whole wall appears as one huge stone. Secondly, the stones are laid together and so perfectly fitted that mortar was not used or required. Next, the walls are constructed in 'Egyptian style', thicker at the bottom.

The walls were quite high, no one knows for sure how high or if the height and dimensions were close to the same as the Temple of Solomon, but the walls were high which added to the majesty of the building. The dressed stone walls were then covered with gold and silver panels. Also, another feature of the Temple of Solomon was the use of precious stones in the decor. Here we also see the use of Emeralds and Turquoise stones. Not as nice as diamonds or rubies or other precious stones, but the best that the local area could produce. We find an interesting double doorway construction at all the important entrances to the various rooms. Also, large 'mantle stones' were placed above the doorways, again a very 'Egyptian style' feature of the construction. The temple had areas for doing sacrifices, washings, and rooms for ordinance work. One of the most beautiful features was the Sun Room or Holy of Holies. This semi circular room is surely the most unique feature of the Temple of Koricancha. Only the high priest officiated here in the Sun room. The roof was constructed of large wood beams covered over with straw or other thatch material to make the roof water proof. All of these unique features of the Temple of Koricancha made Nephi say that his temple was built after the 'manner of the Temple of Solomon.' The temple also had a large courtyard wall surrounding the temple with gardens and fountains adjoining the temple grounds.

Picture #56
Outer wall of the Temple of Koricancha with a large doorway and large lentil stone over the top. Notches cut in the stone were to support the temple door.

Temple Gardens and Fountains

Today, the Temple Garden area is one of the most beautiful areas in the whole city. It is well maintained and planted with many flower borders. Only one fountain still flows from ancient stone pipes. But, the feeling of peace and tranquility in unsurpassed as one visits this special garden. It is truly a refuse in the heart of Cusco where the hustle and bustle of city life goes on all around. Again Garcilaso in his book, *The Incas* says this about the famous gardens and fountains of Koricancha:

"The temple was decorated with five fountains that were fed from five different sources. Their pipes were of solid gold and their stone pillars were covered with either gold or silver, for the sacrifices were washed in these waters. I remember the last of these fountains which was used to water the garden of the convent that the Spaniards established on this sacred ground. One day it stopped working, to the great despair of the Indians who, not knowing where the water came from, were unable to repair it; and the garden dried up, in spite of their desire and their efforts to save it. This only shows how quickly the Indians lost their traditions, since, in the space of forty-two years, there was not one left who could say from whence came the waters that circulated throughout the temple of their god the Sun." Ref 3. p. 79.

"In the time of the Incas, this garden, in which today the convent brothers cultivate their vegetables, was entirely made of gold and silver; and there were similar gardens about all the royal mansions. Here could be seen all sorts of plants, flowers, trees, animals, both small and large, wild and tame, tiny, crawling creatures such as snakes, lizards, and snails, as well as butterflies and birds of every size; each one of these marvels being placed at the spot that best suited the nature of what it represented."

"There were a tall corn stalk and another stalk from the grain they call *quinoa*, as well as other vegetables and fruit trees, the fruits of which were all very faithfully reproduced in gold and silver. There were also, in the house of the Sun, as well as in that of the king, piles of wool made of gold and silver, and large statues of men, women, and children made of the same materials, in addition to storerooms and recipients for storing the grain they called *pirua*, all of which, together, tended to lend greater splendor and majesty to the house of their god the Sun. All of these valuable works were made by the goldsmiths attached to the Temple, from the tribute of gold and silver that arrived every year from all the provinces of the Empire, and which was so great that the most modest utensils used in the temple, such as pots and pans, or pitchers, were also made of precious metals. For this reason, the temple and its service quarters were called Coricancha, which means the place of gold." Ref 3. p. 80.

Picture #57
Famous temple gardens and fountains of the Temple of Koricancha

Special Attributes of the Temple

There are a few other features of the temple that must be discussed. First, two of the existing chambers today, the chamber of the Stars and the Moon that communicate together in a line have polygonal shaped windows high up on the walls between them. When a person stands on a stone in the floor which has been placed there for such a purpose, then you can see

Pictures #58a & 58b
The famous 'eternity windows' of the Temple of Koricancha

228 TEMPLE OF KORICANCHA

through the next rooms. The stone window openings have all been lined up perfectly to give one a sense of looking through eternity. A very interesting view created to give the patron a sense that the windows keep going forever. These windows are famous and can be seen in the adjoining photo. Photo #58a & 58b.

Five Main Chambers of the Temple of the Sun

There were five main chambers of the Temple of Koricancha. These chambers were called by the Incas: the Temple of the Sun, Temple of the Moon, the Temple of the Stars, the Temple of the Rainbow, and the Temple of Lightning and Thunder. All of these chambers existed and the temple was intact and still in use when the conquistadores arrived in 1533 A.D. as witnessed and written down by the Spanish Chroniclers. During the construction of the convent of Santa Domingo it appears that the Rainbow room, Main Altar, and the Lightning and Thunder room were destroyed to obtain building materials for the new church. What remains then of

the original Temple of the Sun are the two chambers of the Moon and the Stars, and then the circular Sun Room. The south and western walls of the church utilized the Sun Room for the walls of its construction. The rest of the convent were built over the top of the Moon and Star chambers not utilizing these walls as part of the building at least in the last reconstruction in 1953. Even though the walls were not used for the Church of Santa Domingo, it did conceal them from the world for many decades, until the recent excavation and restoration for the tourism industry. See the sketches of the Temple of the Sun. Figure #34 & 35.

Figure #34 & 35
Drawings of the sacred Temple of Koricancha

The Sun Room

The most unique feature of the Temple of Koricancha is probably the Sun Room. This semi-circular room is thought to be where the High Priest served and communicated with God. Today the tour guides will point out the Sun Dial features of the room. Shadows are cast down from special stones that have been built into the walls. These shadows tell the time of year and the hour of the day. This information would be useful to the High Priest in his leadership of the people for analysis of planting times and festival days. The construction of perfectly cut Andesite stone in a round building was a very difficult feat. Only a very important and one of a kind building would have such an exquisite feature such as a round room which is considered the most difficult form of Pre-Incan architecture. The round

Picture #59
A close up picture of the unique round exterior wall of the Sun Room.

exterior of the Temple of Koricancha is probably the most recognizable feature of the building. Even with the Church of Santa Domingo built on top of this round room, the Pre-Inca construction was evident for centuries. See photo #59.

The Tunnels of Koricancha

The tunnels underneath the City of Cusco and the Temple of Koricancha have long been of major interest to archeologists and treasure hunters alike. Even from colonial times the Spanish suspected that the Incas hid the majority of their wealth underground in these tunnels and then purposely collapsed them on the arrival of the conquistadors. Lots of rumors and legends still circulate about this immense hidden wealth. However, to date neither the city government or private land owners have cooperated in digging up the streets to ascertain if the ancient stories are true.

The archaeological study, the Wiraccocha Project, conducted recently in Cusco, Peru, shows a system of tunnels which started at the Temple of Koricancha according to Spanish archaeologist, Anselm Pi Rambla. Using modern technology, a method called 'Ground Penetrating Radar' (GPR), this group of scientists from Spain, the 'Bohic Ruz Explorer', have been able to map out this interesting system of tunnels that extend north from the Temple of Koricancha to Sacsahuaman. The entrance appears to be beneath the altar of Santa Rosa, which is the main altar of the temple. This series of tunnels is five meters deep and is of ancient design. It extends from Koricancha to the Plaza de Armas, (Main City Square) and then to the fortress of Sacayhuaman some two kilometers in length. The tunnel links the temple of Koricancha with the Convent of Santa Catalina or Marcahuasi, with the main Cathedral or Temple of Inca Wiraccocha, with the palace of Huascar, with the Temple of Manco Capac or Colcampata, and with the Huamanmarca. All of these buildings are in a perfect astronomical alignment, which confirms that ancient Peruvians also guided their constructions by the location of the Sun, the Moon, and the constellations. See the associated figure #36 of Cusco. Ref 22.

Of course the motivation for such work is the search for the hidden Inca treasure that eluded the Spanish and Pizzarro back in 1533. It has been traditionally thought that the Incas hid the bulk of their temple treasure in a deep nearby lake or possibly buried it to keep it from falling into the hands of the European invaders. These tunnels under Cusco have been abandoned and condemned for centuries and were in disrepair even before the Spaniards arrived. Everyone who entered never returned and died, so the conquistadores sealed up the entrances for safety sake. Anselm Pi, President of Bohic Ruz Explorer has said:

> "We know that the accumulation of metals over a long period of time, in an enclosed and humid space, such as the subsoil of Cuzco can create toxic substances such as cyanide, mercury or chloride. Inhaling these substances is probably what killed explorers in times past. But we enter prepared." Ref 22.

There are for instance stories of explorers over the centuries that have entered the tunnels. One such story tells of a young man who entered, got disoriented, but finally returned to the entrance clutching a cob of corn made of pure gold. He died soon after, presumably poisoned by the dangerous confines of the tunnel. The cob of corn was speculated to have been part of the lost or hidden temple garden treasure. The Catholic priests had the artefact melted down and made into a crown for their bishop. The crown can still be seen on display even today. The entrances to the tunnels either no longer exist or are not accessible to the public, and are now only a legend of the past.

Whether or not the tunnels can be reconstructed and entered using special suits and breathing air is not as important as the artefacts to be recovered. It would be very important for instance if ancient records

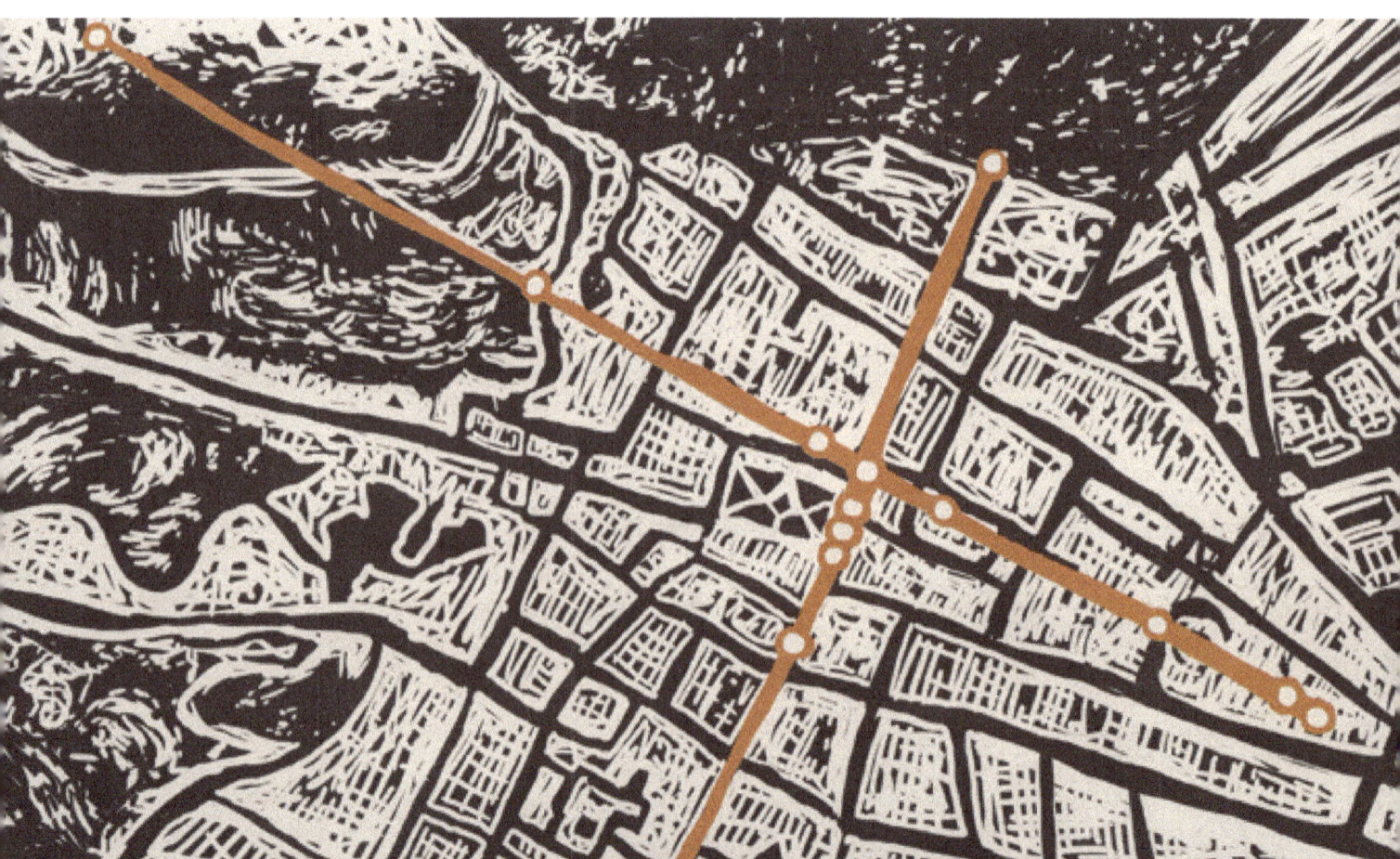

Figure #36 GPR aerial photo of underground tunnel from the Fortress of Sacsauhuaman on hill northwest of city to Temple of Koricancha on the southeast. The other tunnel line bisects the main tunnel at the Plaza de Armas in the center of the city.

could be discovered which would not only prove that the ancient Pre-Inca peoples did have a writing system but also that could collaborate the Book of Mormon writings. King Mosiah I, probably, was able to take most of his records with him to Zarahemla, so to expect any ancient records of the original Nephites is a long shot. However, Limhi and his people left the City of Nephi in haste and the possibility of leftovers of records of his kingdom and era are a better possibility. Such records of course would be an invaluable find that could substantiate the entire work of Joseph Smith and the Restoration.

Picture #60
Outer wall of the Temple of Koricancha shows nibs and holes where golden plates were attached that the conquistadors robbed from the temple in 1533.

Picture #61
Large massive stones exquisitely dressed and fit together without mortar.

The Temple of Koricancha, the Temple of Nephi, was the crowning achievement in the life of the Prophet Nephi. It was embellished and revered by succeeding generations, and maintained its grandeur to colonial times only to be destroyed by the Inquisition and the Spanish invaders of the 16th Century. It is part of the culture and the religion of the Inca even to our modern day. We can rightly say it is still for them, today, the Center of the Universe and the Navel of the World.

THE CITY OF NEPHI 237

{Facing Picture Ch #11} Very unique stone with 12 corners in the ancient fortress.

CHAPTER 11

SUMMARY

In the concluding chapter of this book it would be an injustice to not review at least one of the prophecies of the Book of Mormon and the descendants of Lehi. The prophet Abinadi from the days of the wicked King Noah, who lived in the City of Nephi, tells of the wickedness of the Nephites and that the Book of Mormon would be a testimony against them to other nations:

> 8. And it shall come to pass that except they repent I shall utterly destroy them from off the face of the earth; yet they shall leave a **record** behind them, and I will preserve them for other nations which shall possess the land; yea, even this will I do that I may discover the abominations of this people to other nations. And many things did Abinadi prophecy against this people. Mosiah 12:8

It is evident that the Lord had many purposes for the Book of Mormon and made sure that it would survive and could be translated and available for us in the last days. The Book of Mormon is a testimony of Jesus Christ, of this covenant people of the Lord, and his dealings with his people. It is His warnings and prophecies to this people written for us so that we may learn and benefit from this historical account.

This book, *The City of Nephi,* has been written to bring to life the work of the Prophet Nephi and his city and the temple that he built. We have learned about the legends of the ancient peoples of South America and Manco Capac, Nephi. We have seen how Manco Capac and his brothers journeyed into the wilderness with their sister-wives and families in search of a new land and place where they could prosper and build their city, Cusco, and a temple to God. The legends also rehearse the stories of Wiraccochan (Jesus Christ), how he came to teach and heal the people, then promised to return one day. The natives carved his likeness on a mountain to commemorate and to remember his visit.

This is the very purpose of the Book of Mormon. It is written to the descendants of the family of Lehi that he brought to the Promised Land. It is written that they may remember and be convinced that Jesus Christ is their Lord and Savior. It is written to bring us all to Christ. The Title page of the Book of Mormon states:

> ….Which is to show unto the remnant of the House of Israel what great things the Lord hath done for their fathers; and that they may know the covenants of the Lord, that they are not cast off forever….And also to the convincing of the Jew and Gentile that JESUS is the CHRIST, the ETERNAL GOD, manifesting himself unto all nations… Title Page – Book of Mormon

The Book of Mormon is truly a marvellous work for our day. It was restored by God to the prophet Joseph Smith so that we might benefit from its teachings. Hopefully this book, The City of Nephi, has brought increased faith and testimony of the Book of Mormon, and about the inhabitants of the Americas and the people that are a remnant of the family of Lehi. A thorough study of the Book of Mormon is a key to understanding what the Lord wants us as His covenant people to know in the latter days. It is truly the most correct book ever written on earth.

> Joseph Smith said, "I told the brethren that the Book of Mormon was the most correct of any book on earth, and the keystone of our religion, and a man would get nearer to God by abiding by its precepts, than by any other book."

Picture #62
The natives carved the likeness of Wiraccochan (Jesus Christ) on their mountain so that they would remember Him daily.

By analyzing closely the very words and precepts that are contained in the Book of Mormon we can very clearly see this land and its people, and hopefully make some good conclusions about its geography, archaeology, and history. It helps us explain this ancient record to the world, and flood the earth with the Book of Mormon. That is our sacred responsibility in these last days. These people are real. The city of Cusco, (City of Nephi) really does exist, and the temple that he built to God can still be seen today. These things are available to all people who want to discover the marvels of this mysterious land, and search for them. Don't worry if your search has taken you to Mexico or other lands, as long as the quest has made great discoveries for you; that is what is important. The Book of Mormon is true. These places and these cities and this people really did exist, and the ruins testify of all these things. May your discoveries build your testimony and bring you closer to Christ is our true objective. May we read the Book of Mormon, study, and ponder its pages daily….

THE CITY OF NEPHI

BIBLIOGRAPHY

1. Salazar, Fernando and Edgar *The Sacred Valley of the Incas, Myths and Symbols* 1996 Sociedad Pacaritanpu Hatha p.13-16 and 57-63.
2. Valera, Blas 1590 *Las Costumbres Antiguas del Peru*. Coleccion los Pequenos Grandes Libros de Historia Americana. Serie I, Tomo VIII. Introduccion, adiciones y comentarios de Francisco Loayza, Lima 1945.
3. Garcilaso de la Vega. *The Incas* 1539-1616, translated by Maria Jolas. New York; Grossman Publishers, 1961.
4. Flornoy, Bertrand, *World of the Incas*, New York: Vanguard Press, Inc., 1965
5. Pachacuti Yanqui, Joan de Santacruz, 1613 *Relacion de Antiguedades deste Reyno del Piru. En: Historia de los Incas y Relacion de su Gobierno*. Coleccion de Libros y Documentos referents a la Historia del Peru. Tomo IX (2da. Serie). Lima 1927
6. Cieza de Leon, Pedro 1553 *Segunda Parte de la Cronica del Peru*. Que Trata del Senorio de los Incas Yupanquis y de sus grades hechos y gobernacion. Publicado por Marcos Jimenez de las Espada. Madriz 1880.
7. Little, James A. and Richards, Franklin D. *Compendium* Salt Lake City: Deseret News 1912 edition, but copyright 1882 p. 289
8. Reynolds and Sjodahl, *Book of Mormon Geography* p. 54
9. Pratt, Orson,-- *Remarkable Visions*
10. Dalton, Leon C., *Routes to the Promised Land,* which appeared in the "Liahona", The Elders Journal, August 8, 1944
11. Priddis, Venice, 1975, *The Book and the Map* Bookcraft, Inc. 1975
12. Skousen, W. Cleon, *Treasures From The Book of Mormon* Volume 1 p.1019 "Portrait of Lehi"
13. Heyerdahl, Thor, 1963 *Kon-Tiki* Simon & Schuster 1963
14. Bernand, Carmen, *The Incas – Empire of Blood and Gold* Thames and Hudson New Horizons 1988.
15. Nash, Nathaniel C., *Archaeologist Wants to Reconquer Shrine for Incas* The New York Times 31 August 1993.
16. Cridlin, Erin, *The Native Olmec Indians* Copyright 2002 by PageWise, Inc.
17. J.M.Allen 14th November 2002
18. Dr. Keith Tankard, *The Inca Empire* – S.A. Labrinth
19. Soustelle, Jacques. *The Route of the Incas*. The Viking Press, New York.

20. Brown, Matthew B., *The Gate of Heaven* p.113 Covenant Communications Inc. American Fork, Utah 1999
21. Terrien, Samuel, *The Omphalos Myth and Hebrew Religion*, Vetus Testamentum, vol. 20, no. 3, July 1970, 317
22. Sierra, Javier, First report: Inca Gold, In Search of the Ultimate Sacred Treasure 2001 http://www.grahamhancock.com/forum/SierraJ1-p9.php
23. Sutton, Bruce S., *Lehi, Father of Polynesia – Polynesians are Nephites* Hawaiki Publishing 2001.
24. Kocherhans, Arthur J., *Lehi's Isle of Promise*, 1989 Kobo Enterprises, Placentia, California p.115-119
25. Talmage, James E., *Jesus The Christ*, September 1915, Published by Joseph F. Smith, Trustee-in-Trust for the Church of Jesus Christ of Latter-Day Saints.
26. Heyerdahl, Thor, *Aku-Aku: The Secret of Easter Island*, 1957 -- From Wikipedia, The Free Encyclopedia
27. Lundwall, N.B., *Masterful Discourses and Writings of Orson Pratt*, Bookcraft Inc. 1962, 5th Printing 1981.
28. Pratt, Parley P., *Autobiography of Parley P. Pratt*, Published by Deseret Book in 1874 by his son Parley Parker Pratt after his death in 1857.
29. Cannon, George Q., *The Life of Nephi, the Son of Lehi* (The Contributor Company, Salt Lake City, Utah, 1888 -- full title, *The Life of Nephi, the Son of Lehi, who emigrated from Jerusalem, in Judea, to the land which is now known as South America, about six centuries before the coming of our Savior*).
30. Williams, Frederick Samuel, *The Life of Dr. Frederick G. Williams: Couselor to the Prophet Joseph Smith*, 2012 BYU Studies.
31. Bernhisel, John Milton, *The Bernhisel Manuscript – Copy of Joseph Smith's Inspired Version of the Bible*. BYU Studies 1 (3) Retrieved 29 September 2016.
32. Maugh, Thomas H. II (*February 18, 2009*). "Major cache of fossils unearthed in L.A.". *Los Angeles Times*. Los Angeles

About the Author

L. (Les) Norman Shurtliff, was born in St. George, Utah, and grew up on a small vegetable farm in Southern Nevada where he lived with his parents, four brothers and two sisters. After graduation from high school the family sold the farms in Nevada and moved to Canada. Les was able to serve a mission for the LDS Church in Argentina for two years where he learned the Spanish language and the culture of the wonderful people of South America. He attended Brigham Young University and received a Bachelor of Science Degree in 1979. Immediately after graduation from university the family moved from Vanderhoof, B.C. to the small town of Taylor, B.C. Les got a job at the local oil refinery as a chemist and held various positions there in the lab and in management for the next 25 years. Les and his family also developed a greenhouse complex to grow bedding plants and trees for reforestation. Eventually, Les would venture out on his own and build a gas chromatography lab which was later sold to Norwest Labs. Les managed the Fort St. John Norwest lab for three and a half years and built an environmental lab for the company until it again changed hands and was sold.

After his mission 46 years ago Les was able to visit and see first hand the magical land of the Incas. Intrigued with the history and culture of South America Les has re-visited this land of beauty and mystery many times since and continues to search this 'Promised Land' for its many types of treasure. The gold may now be gone or only found in museums, but there is still other kinds of treasure more important that can only be found in the wonderful people who live in the enchanted Andean Highlands. Les has spent a lifetime studying and visiting South America and has a unique passion for this people and their legends. The evidence of this passion is seen in the long hours and effort to write a series of novels, The Eldorado Series, which will bring to life the story of a chosen and elect people.

Les and his wife, Christal, continue to live in Taylor, B.C., and they have four sons, three daughters and twenty-five grandkids. Les now owns and manages several businesses of his own with his wife as his business partner including the original greenhouse and landscaping business, and a Quiznos Restaurant. His real passion is to visit South America during the cold winter months in Canada and thus escape to a land where dreams really have come true.

www.ingramcontent.com/pod-product-compliance
Lightning Source LLC
Chambersburg PA
CBHW061104070526
44579CB00011B/127